Bicycles and Blisters

Bicycles and Blisters

YHA Memoirs from 1938–84

Margaret E. Whitney

Bicycles and Blisters
Margaret E. Whitney

Published by Aspect Design 2021
Malvern, Worcestershire, United Kingdom.

Designed, printed and bound by Aspect Design
89 Newtown Road, Malvern, Worcs. WR14 1PD
United Kingdom
Tel: 01684 561567
E-mail: allan@aspect-design.net
Website: www.aspect-design.net

ISBN 978-1-912078-01-1

Contents

Where It All Began

Margaret Edith Whitney was born on 30 July 1914 in the King's Norton district of Birmingham. Her parents were Hilda and Edward (Teddy) Whitney. She had an elder sister Hildred who was to become a Good Shepherd nun. Music and her faith played a big part in her life. Her father played the trombone and the piano. She played the violin and joined the City of Birmingham Symphony Orchestra, but was not allowed to take it up as a career as it was deemed to be unsuitable.

She trained as a secretary and worked amongst other things for the director general of the BBC. She was also a legal secretary latterly – working for a solicitor in Rubery. She had a great love of the countryside, and a tremendous sense of adventure which never left her.

The start of the Great Adventure.
Margaret (M) and her friend Dora (D) setting forth on their first trip in 1938.

Out into the Unknown

Thursday 14 April 1938

M and D adjourned after business duties to Lyons' with a view to obtaining nose-bags! They worked themselves up into a state of hysteria waiting for a hopeless waitress to attend to their needy requirements. Eventually they emerged, satisfied, and descended to platform five, Snow Hill Station – great excitement! Got involved with bicycles amidst a hustling holiday crowd. At last the train appeared! With lots of other creatures they rushed for a compartment and found two divine corner seats – placed their luggage on the rack and turned to find two handsome 'pop-eyes' (cyclists) following at the rear. Full of hope! Alas! They had boarded the Stourbridge Local and were soon back on the platform where they first started. Much excitement and great commotion when they discovered that the G.W.R. had excelled themselves once more and they were *even* on the wrong platform. Having remedied this error, they made a frantic dash to, this time, the right train, only to find that all the seats had either been reserved with a penalty of £5 for using them, or occupied by an uproarious mob. Their two handsome pop-eyes, alas, were either Stourbridge locals or luckier than they were in obtaining seats – hopeless!

After much commotion they ended up in an absolutely unprofitable compartment containing only pop-eyes whom they decided, were entirely out of the question. Their light heartedness and general conversation seemed to cause great amusement amongst the half-soaked occupants thereof. However, they were fortunate enough to get rid of these at Wolverhampton where they all filed out. Great relief on their part – hope reigning for better things to come! But no! They now found themselves faced with· a loud-voiced accented creature of the feline species who would persist in being voluble; another, after the once-over, thought to be a murderer, but who later loaned them his pencil wherewith to write these memoirs; and a gay Irishman on his way to Dublin – complete with bicycle and paper carrier.

They gracefully withdrew from the conversation leaving the loud-voiced female and Taffy to carry on a mild flirtation, while they devoured the aforementioned nose-bags and admired the passing countryside. (Much giggling on their part.) The woman, however, made her exit at Shrewsbury and they were once again confronted with another hopeless multitude.

By this time, having set eyes on no suitable pop-eyes, they decided to walk up the corridor and gracefully faint outside a compartment calling for romance, but were discouraged from this procedure by more conversation on the part of the Irishman.

On arrival at Gobowen there was much shouting of 'Change for Llangollen!' Anxiety was caused by the lackadaisical manner of a hopeless porter in extracting their cycles from the mass of debris in the guard's van. Also great confusion and general embarrassment in proffering 6d for the said services rendered. Having surmounted this awkward situation they leapt into the midst of an H.F. party also travelling to Llangollen – seven in all – and travelled with this jolly crowd for the rest of the journey amidst great hilarity, and with the hope that their bicycles were safely following in the rear. They suddenly became aware of the fact that a 'fortyish' pop-eye, whom they had noticed at Snow Hill, was sitting near them and taking a very active interest in them. They did their 'stuff' and succeeded eminently.

The scenery from Gobowen consisting of hills and valleys, with setting sun in the background, making a wonderful panorama. (They had to ask a further pop-eye for the loan of a pencil wherewith to continue these memoirs.) More shouting at this point of 'Change for Llangollen!' Great surprise and exclamation on their part!

They alighted from the train only to find that there was no sign of the guard's van in the next train. Much running up and down platform to find same. Eventually discovered this in the middle of the train and travelled down with the H.F. crowd in an unlighted carriage to Llangollen.

They arrived at 9.15 p.m., and with other hikers, cyclists and mountain climbers, fought their way out of the station and proceeded towards the hostel. Here they were greeted by a Scotch lass – Kinna – and were transported up to room one to gaze on bunk upon bunk – entirely without hope – and, after depositing essentials, wandered forth in an aimless fashion, finding their way into the common room feeling very self-conscious!

However, having moved in and out about half-a-dozen times they decided that they had better not appear again and leapt upstairs only to find, much to their amazement and amusement, that they were in the men's quarters – fated!

They rushed down again after this discovery and into the

common room once more, regardless of all occupants. This time they were invited by a Liverpool pop-eye, in quaint garb, to take a seat by the fire. The time 10.30 p.m., when all lights should have been out. After polite conversation they retired to room one amidst hopeless females, to find that one fat ancient 'piece' was already in repose, complete with curlers, on one bottom bunk. They proceeded to make beds, getting very involved with sleeping bag tapes, and eventually climbed up and crawled in to the accompaniment of much creaking. What a night! People wandering about till the early hours of the morning – lambs bleating – river rushing – and above all, frozen to the marrow! First words on waking:

D: (peering to lower bunk in a state of semi-collapse)
'Did you sleep well?'
M: (also in state of semi-collapse – emerging from blankets)
'No!'
D: 'Neither did I,' and then –
M: 'Did you feel warm?'
D: (settling into blankets again)
'No!'
M: 'Neither did I.'
Hopeless and fated!

Breakfast bell at 7.15 a.m. found them getting ready to pack their bikes. The bathroom was over-flowing with enthusiastic neck and ear washers. They, however, did not belong to this category.

Many wanderings and good mornings until breakfast was served. Collected their own porridge and adjourned to the dining room to consume same. Likewise, bacon and egg, bread and butter and marmalade. Afterwards, being charged with the duty of cleaning the aforementioned dining room – once more fated!

Nine o'clock saw them floating down the road in the direction of Corwen accompanied by the aforesaid Liverpool pop-eye (still in quaint garb) with whom they were very well in; his parting remark being, 'See you again soon, girls.'

They passed through some marvellous scenery with wonderful views until they came to a very expensive-looking hotel, and being in a famished condition, and quite regardless of the outrageous bill with which they thought they should be presented, marched up importantly to the front entrance where they were greeted by an Irishwoman, quite charming, and seeming to know their every need.

A subdued and timid-looking maid (in this condition, no doubt, due to their appearance) directed them to the bathroom which they found after roaming through countless corridors. They glided down, in a refreshed state, to a dinner which consisted of: plaice, peas, bread and butter, pot of tea (in silver teapot) and fruit salad and cream (plenty of it) all for the surprisingly modest sum of 1/10d per head. They would here mention that great difficulty was experienced in understanding the dialect of the said maid, who spoke at 120 words per minute in Welsh. The only remark they apprehended being, 'Enough bread and butter, yes – no?'

At two o'clock they once more set out on their journey, colliding at the gate with four black pop-eyes just going in for lunch – lucky chaps! They rode for fifteen minutes and parked in a most glorious spot, lying full length on the grass for two hours – a most divine siesta – the sun really scorched them as they lay there. By this time they were wholly unrecognisable wearing scarves round their heads and sun-glasses, but this was for the best, no doubt, as they desired to pass departmental cars unnoticed.

Four o'clock found them at Pentre Voleas where M made

a hopeless faux pas! On espying a small stores and desiring to purchase postcards, M approached a prosperous-looking merchant who was standing outside the said stores and enquired, 'Do you sell picture postcards?' to which the said stranger replied, 'I don't come from this part of the country.'

Hopeless laughter on the part of D but complete unconsciousness on the part of M.

They later discovered that the aforementioned merchant was the possessor of a marvellous car and, no doubt, moneyed!

They visited Fairy Glen and Vale of Lledr and then adjourned to Bettws-y-Coed, where they walked into an extremely posh hotel (dinner at seven) looking complete wrecks. They had a good tea in a spacious room, surrounded by decorated tables laid most precisely for dinner. They expected to see Society! Great agitation on their part as they were hardly dressed for the occasion! Waitresses were sounding gongs and rushing forth! The only thing missing to complete the picture being the diners who had not even arrived half-an-hour after the gong had sounded – much to their relief. Fortune favoured them – but not the proprietors.

Marvellous ride to Llanrwst Hostel. Setting sun and mountains making the picture like a miniature Switzerland. They espied the youth hostel perched on top of a mountain! Arrived at the top, breathless and panting, to find that the cycle shed was a further quarter-mile up the mountain – fated! First appearance in hall – leapt upon by most attractive pop-eye who said, 'I have seen you before on the road today.'

M: 'I don't think so.'

D: (telling a hopeless lie) 'Yes, I saw you. (Well in after this.)

They were told by the warden that they were only allowed

two blankets, so after previous night's experience were prepared to acquire icicles!

All the people there were most friendly and they retired to the common room to study map and write memoirs, only to be interrupted by the aforementioned pop-eye, who seated himself, introduced them to further pop-eyes, and an animated conversation on Scotland ensued – two of the pop-eyes being Scotch. The result of this conversation was that they definitely decided never to go youth hostelling in Scotland as they had to cook their own meals. Great surprise when said attractive pop-eye announced 'tea and biscuits' and they adjourned to the dining room which was chock-full of males. (Full of hope.)

The warden informed everyone that it was 10.30 p.m. Their pop-eyes did not appear anxious to move and thus they were the last to retire. This night, despite the fact that they were only allowed two blankets, proved more successful than the first. M sleeping, this time, on the top bunk.

D was awakened by a couple of legs dangling from above, apparently belonging to M. They packed their saddle bags and proceeded to breakfast to find that the aforementioned pop-eye, who had previously informed them of his intention to make an early start without breakfast, was in evidence and had saved them two seats. (Again full of hope.)

Great excitement when bread, butter and marmalade got involved with remains of bacon and egg. Conversation with attractive pop-eye was, by this time, somewhat exhausted and, therefore, painful silences ensued. However, before leaving the breakfast table, he announced that he would see them later.

The warden gave the jobs out! M and D conveniently had one

between them. D later was severely ticked off and humiliated before countless pop-eyes and the hostel in general, and slouched off in dire disgrace, with crimson face, to do the washing-up, but cheered up on discovering that she was the only girl amongst eight pop-eyes. (Hope still in the ascendant.)

M meanwhile retired sheepishly to the bedroom to get on with her job. Met an attractive pop-eye on landing who asked if they were ready to start, as he was, and they obviously came to the conclusion that the early start had been postponed on their account. They wandered down for cycles – wandered back again – meandered up and down stairs – in and out of hostel – round the garden – pumped up tyres, several times – packed saddle bags at least thrice – but still no sign of pop-eye. Feeling thoroughly cheap they at last set out, the time being 9.45 – hopeless!

However, on the road they were overtaken by half-a-dozen members of the male species from the hostel who seemed anxious for their company. In order not to appear 'novices' they rushed along frantically negotiating hills, until, on arrival at the Swallow Falls they fell off their bikes in a state of complete exhaustion and total collapse, with legs trembling violently and palpitations of the heart!

It might here be mentioned that D had contracted a strained joint which prevented free movement of her right leg. Having suffered quite enough for one day, they successfully lost the hopeless crowd, and were unsuccessful in tracing the wandering pop-eye, so ventured along at their own pace towards Llanberis. Here they were overtaken by two fresh pop-eyes from the hostel and had great difficulty in ridding themselves of these – one belonged to the air force, they learnt. Decided that pop-eyes were convenient at hostels but not *en route*! Had a fine journey to Portmadoc when once more, the fun began. (At this juncture the attractive pop-eye had still not caught them up and they spent the day feeling they had played a dirty trick and wondering if he was still waiting for them at the hostel.)

They had now to find lodgings at Portmadoc! Having wandered at great length through the town they became known to all the Portmadoc police force and were followed with suspicious glances – fated!

After this procedure they decided to spend the night at Borth-y-Gest so on they went – up hill – down hill – through hedges – over ditches – across golf courses – over hopeless roads – eventually coming to the sea shore and a wide stretch of sand. They came to the conclusion that if they proceeded forth along the sands they should eventually arrive at Borth-y-Gest. However, it was a great error on their part. After negotiating quick-sands and nearly losing sight of their bikes therein, paddling through pools and clambering over rocks, they were informed that it was impossible to proceed further without drowning and that they should have to return the way they had come. They almost decided to drown! By this time their spirits were at zero and D, showing marked evil tendencies lapsed into stony silence, while M, endeavouring to be bright (with great effort) produced chocolates and kept up a cheery conversation but entirely without effect. D still remained evil and found it difficult to proceed with half of Borth-y-Gest sand in her shoes, and with the added encumbrance of a maimed limb. It was now seven o'clock – they had had no tea, and no lodgings for the night were in view! Hot and breathless they returned to the road at Borth-y-Gest, and dithered on the threshold of a likely abode, only to decide that they – after all – preferred Portmadoc – three miles back the way they had come – hopeless!

At this point they decided that it would be a good idea to draw up a specification, embodying the qualifications required for a good night's rest and they proceeded with forms of tender and form of guarantee to be filled in by two approved sureties.

After mowing up and down the main· street of Portmadoc for at least half an hour they espied a CTC (Cycling Touring Club) which they had passed at least half-a-dozen times without noticing. They timidly approached the door (being ignorant of the correct procedure) only to find that their fears were totally groundless and they were shown a heavenly feather-bed, much appreciated after YHA bunks.

After making it their business to find out if there were any pop-eyes staying there, they wandered in search of what was, by this time, a much needed meal, both possessing aching voids. D, making a hopeless faux pas outside the chemists' shop, much to the amusement of the Saturday night crowds. They glided into what looked like a promising restaurant, but seeing a few dirty table-cloths, wandered out again! They then floated into a fish and chip saloon and had great difficulty in making themselves understood, owing to their complete ignorance of the Welsh language. They here dined on fish, chips and peas (eaten with two forks – rather difficult to negotiate) for the sum of 6d, for which cash had to be proffered on delivery. Meandered forth once more to buy Turkish delights, whipped cream walnuts, and apples for consumption in bed.

At this point they decided to retire early owing to their strenuous day's toil. D had great difficulty in leaping into bed owing to still stiff limb. Spent a marvellous night with the luxury of an eiderdown, and proceeded to breakfast, meeting over bacon and eggs, two further pop-eyes. A cheery atmosphere reigned – to be somewhat marred by the grumblings of a hopelessly pessimistic husband and wife. (They might here mention that the saddle bags were not adequate for their needs – desperate efforts having to be made each day to cram in all the required articles. M getting jumper sleeve involved in back wheel, while D had scarf dangling dangerously in chain.)

They went to church and then on to Harlech where they had a marvellous meal near the castle with the sea in view. Having negotiated several level crossings, toll gates, etc., with much confusion, (D showing marked knowledge of manipulating these and getting in well with all the keepers thereof) they arrived at Barmouth.

They settled on the beach to write these memoirs when they were rudely interrupted by the arrival of two very spruce and well-to-do town pop-eyes. Much excitement and confusion but they eventually settled down with one on either side of them, aimlessly throwing stones the while, and to eventually rid themselves of these they were forced to introduce two boys named Geoffrey and Stan into the conversation, accompanied by other bits of exaggeration. They proceeded onward unattended as they said they had to meet these at Dolgelley. Arrived at Tea Place – big affair – at Barmouth – only to be met on the step by an eager business 'piece' who told them that they were full up but that there was room at The Moorings. Proceeded to make a hurried exit but M, overcome by a sudden brain-storm, exclaimed that they only wanted tea. At this juncture they were welcomed with

open arms and escorted in. After a wash and brush up they sat
down to the plainest tea they had yet set eyes on. This was eaten
to the accompaniment of incessant chattering on the part of the
proprietress, in an endeavour to promote business. They were
duly presented with visiting cards, D being left to carry on polite
conversation while M retired, behind a curtain, in speechless,
but not silent, laughter. Hopeless for D as may well be imagined.

   After being ushered off the premises they proceeded towards
Dolgelley feeling that they could put away a good square meal.
However, they free-wheeled down and struggled up hills until
they eventually arrived at the youth hostel – three miles at least up
the mountain pass – Cader Idris. This path ascended by a rushing
torrent and D and M were continually attracted to the valley below
– riding perilously near the edge. M, in an endeavour to know if they
were on the correct road approached a youth, obviously studying
for holy orders, while D collapsed in the background! They arrived
at the hostel and were met by a hale and hearty warden, who knew
all about them – names etc. – before being told. They arrived at the
conclusion that he belonged to the supernatural! Met Fanny the
Second, ticking off everbody, with ready smiles for males, and who,
amidst the silence of the common room, made much of her travels,
the only absent features being rolling tears, and tongue in action.
They retired to bed in a state of starvation, hoping to live through
the night! They would at this point mention that their wrinkles
were very deep owing to the sun, but grey hairs had disappeared.
Were put right by the warden, who told them that they looked like
juniors. Greatly flattered! D was extremely fortunate in procuring
four blankets, M, being less lucky, and further more was perched
near a window over a 'piece', who complained next morning at

breakfast regarding M's restlessness. D found a bed near the door not setting eyes on upper 'fragment'. Great commotion ensued next morning when someone rose at 6.30 a.m. thinking it was 7. 30 a.m. Fated! Descended to breakfast, both in a half-starved condition, thinking of nothing but food.

Decided, after saying good bye to the sea last night, to return that morning, involving another twenty-mile journey but they felt so invigorated that that was a mere nothing. Sea was a lovely blue, and sky too! The view was so marvellous that they were quite overcome! They should not forget in a hurry the splendour of this country! Bought scones and chocolate and parked near the sea. Afterwards journeying onward, M discovering that she had left the map on the sea wall. Further fated and quite hopeless! They regained same and proceeded along the coast road until they turned inland to Taly-llyn Lake. Here things were not so good.

Being in a state of famine they had to stop at the one and only Hotel at Taly-llyn, and there entered the spacious dining-room looking anything but the part; feasted like kings and paid accordingly! Not being able to afford a tip, they made their exit through the window, and beat a hasty retreat, struggling along the side of the lake as the wind was against them.

Spent all afternoon on climbing about five hundred feet, and gradually got more and more evil as the day wore on. They decided to sit on the side of the road and salute what may have been departmental cars. Proceeded onward down the hill to Brithdir where they had tea in the front garden of a tea-house – still on view for the benefit of departmental cars. D, showing very business-like tendencies, approached the back door saying to the obviously new-at-the-game proprietress, 'Can I settle with you now?'

Reply: 'Oh, yes! It is over there!' Hopeless and much audible laughter on the part of D and M. They then felt it their duty then to 'go over there'.

Commenced the ascent to Bala, doing business on the way with a YHA bound youth who lent them a map which they did not require. On nearing the hostel, and not being certain of the way D approached what proved to be a most voluble Welshman – indeed to goodness, yes, who seemed far more interested in international problems of the day than the right road to the hostel. D and M alternately blew noses vigorously to hide laughter. Here arrived two more pop-eyes who relieved the tension and accompanied them to the hostel.

First conclusion drawn

That the place was pre-historic and had not had a 'wash and brush-up' since the sixteenth century – fated once more!

They approached nervously to discover that the place was shrouded in darkness, the only sign of life being one ghostly phantom half-way up the stairs, who turned to them with a glassy stare and snapped 'have you booked? Increased terror of D and M. After some minutes of complete silence, they were lead to a dark and eerie room, which later proved to be the office of this individual. They were asked to sign a book and at this juncture, noticed that he was obviously 'under the influence of drink'. By this time they had definitely decided that this nasty piece of work was no less than a murderer and, no doubt there were several bodies in the house.

They were directed to a bedroom, but owing to numerous long and dark passages, curtained alcoves, sliding panels, etc., they were now terrified to go on without a lamp, and so returned, to be met by another glassy stare. Complete with storm lamp throwing weird shadows around them, they once more roamed the corridors, accompanied by a far distant sinister whistle – that of the murderer! Finding that they were the only inmates of a huge and much alcoved bedroom, with latticed windows, they were too petrified to think of remaining. M suggested bed and breakfast in Bala, D suggested moving into the next room which was already full! Being in such a state of nervous agitation they adopted the latter suggestion and removed beds from the empty bedroom. They then meandered forth into the silent night to the cycle shed. In quite a hopeless state now, they hurried back to the front door, only to find that they were locked out! Banged, pushed, kicked, shoved and knocked, and after about ten minutes, a female spectre glided to the door, opening same and totally ignoring their bright conversation. They were then informed that the place was haunted, that a murder had taken place there and that every night a woman's scream was heard resounding through the building. At this point they adjourned to the common room, which was wrapped in silence, in a state of total collapse, and to the accompaniment of haunting music which floated through the house. This room was decorated with knights of armour on the walls, antique furniture, carvings etc. There were at least ten occupants, obviously all in much the same state as themselves. They bore this for about half-an-hour and in desperation retired to bed, after filling the other occupants with fear and dread, preparing for a sleepless night. They scurried along to the bathroom and emerged to observe a female phantom, stealthily negotiating the corridor outside the bedroom – very fishy.

D awaited the dawn in a cramped condition unable, due to fright, to manipulate a turn-over. M slept the sleep of the just. However, morn duly arrived, bringing with it M and D free from harm. Breakfast was served by two half-wits (Welsh) while the murderer lurked in the background. They were now able to take a good look at same in daylight – tall and thin, sunken eyes, hollow cheeks, ragged hair, unshaven face, looking as though he had been dressed thus since the sixteenth century. They decided from his shifty look and fishy manner that he was weighed down by an unclear conscience. However, in daylight M and D faced the situation that the poor man was trying to be pleasant without success! One thing in his favour, owing to his lackadaisical manner, M and D escaped all duties and proceeded 'jobless' on their way – thankful to be alive!

They were so early in starting, due to lack of duties, that they were frozen so stopped for 'keep fit classes', and later a cup of tea. Decided at this point not to go evil on entering civilisation, and had a good lunch in Llangollen. Caused great excitement amongst civilians owing to their sunburnt countenances which showed up amongst the anaemics! Hopeless waitress who was a 'pardonnibus' came to attend to them. They ordered spaghetti on toast and were much amused when she repeated the order saying 'two forget-me – nots on toast for bofe'. Were very surprised to find 'fortyish' pop-eye, whom they had met on the downward journey in Café who haled them like old friends and said that he would look out for them on the homeward train. Showed them snaps he had taken and they generally concluded that they were well in. Whilst eating their lunch they encountered a 'Miss Barnwell the second' who did much batting of eyelids with affected movement. Their stockings by this time were merely held together with bits of soap and face cream so they purchased a fresh pair each and entered civilisation respectable, at least as far as their legs were concerned. Decided to cycle to Ruabon and catch an earlier connection from Chester thus missing – unfortunately – 'fortyish'. They purchased tea to consume on the train and wandered to the station. Here again much embarrassment on the part of D in proffering tips to porter looking after bicycles, but being very well in after doing so, and being told that cycling was the best exercise for the nervous system. (After their experience at the haunted house at Bala they thought this all to the good).

The journey homeward was definitely more interesting than the outward one as, no sooner had they boarded the train than two pop-eyes leapt up to make room for them. They afterwards regained other seats in the same compartment and carried on a lively conversation. They arrived at the conclusion that one – M's – was a doctor and that D's was a barrister. It may well be imagined how disappointed they were when they steamed into Snow Hill Station and had to say good-bye as they were continuing their journey to London. Much waving as the train drew out – absolutely hopeless, hopeless, hopeless! Completely fated and doomed!

Easter 1938

		Expenditure	Sub-total
Thursday 14 April 6.15pm. train from Snow Hill to Llangollen arriving 9.15pm. Cycled about one mile to youth hostel.	Fare Tea Tip	15s.6d 6d 6d	16s.6d
Friday 15 April: 44 miles. Llangollen – Corwen – Bettws-y- Coed – Llanrwst.	B&B Dinner Tea	2s.0d 1s.10d 1s.0d	4s.10d
Saturday 16 April: 50 miles Llanrwst – Bettws-y-Coed – Swallow Falls – Llanberis Pass – Beddgelert – Aberglaslyn Pass – Portmadoc.	B&B P/d lunch Horlicks Supper	2s.0d 6d 5d 6d	3s.5d
Sunday 17 April: 31 miles Portmadoc – Penrhyndeudraeth – Harlech – Barmouth – Dolgelly.	B&B Dinner Tea	4s.6d 1s.6d 1s.0d	7s.0d
Monday 18 April: 50 miles Dolgelly – Fairbourne – Llyngwril – Rhoslefain – Taly-llyn – Brithdir – Bala.	B&B Lunch Dinner Tea	2s.3d 5d 3s.0d 1s.0d	6s.8d
Tuesday 19 April: 36 miles Bala – Corwen – Llangollen – Ruabon	B&B Dinner Pot tea Tea	2s.0d 1s.7d 4d 8d	4s.7d
	Sundries	7s.6d	7s.6d
Total mileage: 215 miles	Total		£2.10s.6d

Going West

September 1939

Arrived at Snow Hill Station both feeling they could not stand Birmingham a minute longer. With frayed nerves and worried expressions they scoured up and down the aforementioned station in search of M's mother (who was in possession of M's money) only to find, after a quarter of an hour had expired that she was viewing them from a far distant seat, placidly chewing and quite oblivious of their obvious state. In a calm manner, foreign to M and D, they surveyed the train with a view to corner seats, getting involved with a devoted mother leaving her loving son, who would persist in pushing backwards and forwards in the corridor. Bade good bye to parents who wore worried looks and 'never see you again' expressions on their faces.

The journey to Bristol was more or less uneventful, apart from a 'bundle of nerves' who would persist in rushing in and out of the corridor and leaping forth on the seat, clutching luggage feverishly meanwhile. At the next stop after Cheltenham M and D, without a thought as to whether they had reached their proper destination, calmly made their exit from the train, procured bikes from guard's van, there being no porter in sight, and not

until the train had steamed out did they realise that they were
at a small branch station at Bristol with ten miles to cycle.

This ten miles seemed to consist mainly of up hills with
cobbled streets, and hopeless trams, buses, etc. After getting
involved with countless policemen, they were directed through
Bristol and eventually arrived at Cabot House (their abode for
the night) in a breathless state feeling definitely the worse for
wear. This proved to be a palatial building standing in its own
grounds and several storeys high, but owing to the lateness of
the hour, all was shrouded in darkness. The proprietress, who
had by this time quite given up hope of ever seeing them that
night, was just in the act of bolting the door when they made
their entrance. They were invited to take their bikes into the
spacious hall and they sank inches deep in carpets and brushed
against the palms. They were made comfortable with a pot of
tea and biscuits and were then escorted to their bedroom. They
were shown into a moonlit room containing – two wardrobes,
washstand, dressing-table, bureau, two cabinets, table, settee,
double bed, three chairs and numerous trunks; upon one of
which rested the 'NIGHT MUST FALL' trunk, exactly similar in all
respects to the one in the film, which contained the head of some
unfortunate party whom M and D were sure had been murdered
in that very room. After investigating all the furniture, looking
under the bed and hiding from sight the aforementioned leather
box, they tremblingly retired to bed, with curtains drawn back
and windows thrown open, thus allowing the moon to penetrate
the room, especially D's pillow. Poor D! After lying in silence and
agony, listening to weird and ghostly noises for two hours, each
thinking the other was asleep, D frantically clutched M, who

was quite wide awake, and said that she could not live a moment longer without the light. M, who adopted a very courageous attitude, told D that everything was all right and that she had not heard anything, but it transpired later that she had spent the night so far with fingers in ears and eyes shut tight in fear and trembling. (No wonder she didn't hear or see anything.) It took quite half-an-hour for them both to get out of bed and put on the light. The trouble was that weird noises were being emitted from one of the wardrobes, groans from the direction of the leather box, and flickering lights all over the room which could not be explained. However, at a courageous moment they rushed to the light, drew the curtains and locked the windows and spent the rest of the night with the electric light on, but still to the accompaniment of weird noises. D's temperature rose to 105 °F. Even in the light of day the sounds could not be accounted for. Poor M had complained to D many times amidst the terrors of the night that she had a sore throat and to D's horror the first thing that M did on rising in the morning was to take a dose from a medicine bottle labelled 'quinine' which (in such a murderous atmosphere) would be more likely to contain arsenic. D could plainly see herself figuring in a court scene, giving details of M's rash action and the results of same.

The previous night they had asked to be called at 8 a.m. but at 9 a.m. were still in bed and entirely ignored. They came to the conclusion that they were not expected for a moment to survive the terrors of the night. The fishy looks of the proprietress definitely confirmed their suspicions in the morning. However, they were given a nice breakfast and did very good business with two retired colonels meanwhile, and departed for the boat amidst many promises of help if they should need same, and after having their photographs taken by one of the colonels.

Although having received minute details of the direction to be taken to reach the boat, both M and D had listened and not heard and so on turning the first corner, they once again hailed a pedestrian to enquire the way.

They carefully chose a seat at the front of the boat in order to get the full benefit of any motion. A few hours later they wished they had not been so rash. D, in the company of everyone else was hanging over the side of the boat and M was slowly turning the colour of parchment. While they were supporting each other, and endeavouring to ignore all outside influences, one middle-aged gentleman (who they decided was a teacher), would persist in narrating the full history of every cursed place along the coast giving full details of the legends thereof. M and D were forced to say 'Really – yes and no' with their eyes closed and their minds one complete blank as far as legends were concerned. However, when he realised their physical infirmities, he had the grace to offer soda water and tea which were refused as M and D felt it would involve them in further conversation. At this juncture they both felt very embarrassed in his presence, as only a minute previously he had remarked that they were extraordinarily good sailors. Immediately after this remark they both felt sick.

Ilfracombe was reached amidst pouring rain, and evil tendencies were well to the fore with both M and D. These were appeased a little by baked beans on toast and cakes, but they returned again with full force when M and D were struggling uphill in further rain towards Barnstaple, and a very strained atmosphere pervaded. Needless to say, no note was made of the surrounding country. They might just as well have been climbing up Bradford Street.

On passing a very superior looking hotel, D in her agitation announced that she was staying the night there, totally regardless of the bill with which she would doubtless be confronted with in the morning. M rather unwillingly accompanied her, and to give them time to definitely make up their minds to stay the night they ordered a pot of tea, although D had already commenced unpacking her night clothes. In the meantime, their wet and dripping capes made running rivulets all over the floor. The pot of tea arrived and M and D believed to this day that they *did* consume it, but they were so evil and worried that they were not really sure about this fact, nor how much they paid for same. They enquired about spending the night but although the house was quite empty the proprietors did not seem at all keen on having M and D with them. After much beating about the bush M and D decided to proceed onwards, although the storm had not abated.

They rushed forward and eventually came to a humble-looking abode when D once more announced that she was staying there for the night and would go no further. Just as they were disputing the point a 'piece' arrived to promote business for her friend who was shopping in Barnstaple, and before M and D knew where they were they were sitting in their undies before a blazing fire endeavouring to keep up a cheerful flow of conversation. They retired to bed early, complete with oil lamp, and went to sleep to the accompaniment of torrential rain. On waking M leapt out of bed in the hope that the sun was shining, but clouds still hovered around and the roads were very wet. She then proceeded back to bed, climbing over D, and lifting her eyes to the picture above her, read:

> Sweet and gentle are thy ways
> Oh glorious, beauteous autumn days.

Hopeless!

They lay in bed and debated as to whether they should remain for breakfast, but on opening the bedroom door, they found all their out-of-door garments reposing in a heap on the floor and obviously came to the conclusion that they were expected to proceed without breakfast. However, on arriving downstairs they were provided with a cup of tea and two slices of bread and butter, which they consumed standing up in the scullery.

M and D then went on their way to Barnstaple, the weather being better than the previous night, and here they stopped to have a cup of chocolate which was so hot that it burnt their mouths. They then decided to go to their respective churches and M tootled off to Mass, while D proceeded to the parish church, both looking cuts amongst the well-dressed citizens of this town. D promised to meet M at a given point after the service. M arrived in the middle of her service, it being 10.30 a.m. instead of 11.00 a.m., while poor D arrived at the end. D, not knowing that M's service was over at 11.15 and having it in mind to write to her mother, proceeded towards some gardens and settled herself comfortably until twelve o'clock.

M, meanwhile adjourned to a cafe to fill up the time eating a ham sandwich and drinking a cup of coffee, thinking that D's service was over at about 12.30 p.m.

However, after wasting about an hour looking for each other, they proceeded together towards Bideford and there made themselves thoroughly common by eating scones and cream in a shelter in the main High Street overlooking the river. Having finished these and feeling very much better, they sped forth towards Westward Ho! arriving there at about 3.30 p.m., only to find a forbidding notice on the door of the hostel informing them that cycles were parked at Owner's Risk and that the wardens must not be disturbed until five o'clock. Poor M and D. Not wishing to break any regulations, and, still further, not wanting all their worldly goods stolen, they proceeded down to the beach with bikes and thoroughly investigated Westward Ho!

At 5.15 p.m. they tremulously approached the hostel once more, which, incidentally, was part of Rudyard Kipling's college, and timidly knocked about six times without success, coming to the conclusion that the hostel was shut for the winter, and that it would mean bed and breakfast in Westward Ho! However when loud rumblings were heard from the interior and amidst much pulling back of rusty bolts, the door was slowly opened to reveal the warden – afterwards christened Mephistopheles on account of his fox and devil-like countenance. After surveying them for quite five minutes on the doorstep, they were invited in, complete with bikes and led up countless stairs to the office. It turned out that he knew Moseley quite well, and M and D thought it fit and proper to adopt the Moseley accent, which seemed to create the right impression. There were two other people staying at the hostel and the meals were absolutely scrumptious. That night the warden asked if they would care to have a game of table tennis. They enthusiastically said 'Yes', but after the table had been fixed he invited the only youth present to play with him and it was monopolised until M and D retired to bed. It might be mentioned that on one occasion he enquired if they would like a game, but as his fox-like eyes hypnotised them, they refused without knowing why and later attributed this to the hypnotism.

A marvellous view was enjoyed from the bedroom window right across the Atlantic and the roar of the sea could be heard all night. D, in an effort to reach the top bunk, stood on a chair which over-balanced, immediately throwing her heavily in the direction of the floor. Poor D!

D showed great forethought with regard to blowing up tyres when setting off next morning although she had not the knack of doing it as M had. However, this duty accomplished they set off for Bude Hostel, via Clovelly. They made a detour to Bucks Mills – a most picturesque fishing village – consuming the white chocolate, which caused D great embarrassment at a later date by giving her violent hiccoughs.

The next place visited was Clovelly, one of the most lovely spots, and due to the tourists, being definitely upper-class, M and D thought it wise to adopt an accent, which seemed to be the right thing to do. However, on reaching the top of Clovelly High Street, they went thoroughly common and bought an ice-cream cornet, consuming same along the road feeling most confused and embarrassed on encountering a Salvation Army

gathering in the middle of the road, and not knowing whether
to look intelligent or continue eating ice cream. However, they
pretended they had not observed this meeting and were followed
with disapproving glances and shouts of 'Do you want to be
saved?' M and D, not seeing the point, went on their way.

Owing to the lateness of the hour, and wishing to partake
of the evening meal, they sped along the main road, negotiating
hills at a furious rate. *En route* they decided that they had better
get a stock of chocolate and fruit in case of 'night starvation',
and proceeded into a likely looking store. They were completely
ignored, despite the fact that there were three assistants in the
shop, and so decided, in view of the rudeness shown, to depart.
This they did and were not even called back. However, they met
with success lower down the road. In mentioning that hills were
negotiated at a furious rate it might be stated that D felt very
much more superior than she did at Easter, owing to the low
bicycle she now possessed and both M and D were saved much
confusion owing to the fact that they each possessed two saddle
bags – one containing night things only – and could remove
this latter instead of entering the hostel with all their night
requirements draped about them and dangling on the floor.

Before reaching Bude Hostel they encountered a very steep
hill on Bursden Moor which was really too much for them and
they were happily walking up same, deep in conversation (as
usual) smiling at every passing human form, when a cheery voice
said from behind, 'Do you mind if I walk along with you for a
while?' M and D looked round in astonishment and recognised
an RAC man whom they had previously smiled at, and owing to
their previous friendly spirit, felt they could not ignore him on

this occasion, and a lively conversation ensued. After standing about half-an-hour with this gentleman, who introduced them meanwhile to a colleague on the road, who seemed anxious for 6d of dark at the pictures that same night, M and D decided that still waters run deep.

After this interruption they sped along more quickly than ever and arrived in a breathless state at Bude Hostel, to be confronted by ten pop-eyes and one female. This suited M and D very well and they spent a most enjoyable evening. This hostel was very cheery, in fact M and D concluded that it was a bit too cheerful as from 7 p.m. until 10 p.m. there was ceaseless singing and humming on the part of one of the sisters in charge of the hostel and M and D came to the conclusion that she had been an Opera Singer in her day. However, the food was lovely there and everything else too.

M and D retired to bed at about ten o'clock leaving on the electric light for the benefit of the party who was expected in at any minute. As they had both climbed on to a top bunk the light was left on rather longer than it should have been and they both eventually fell asleep. D, suddenly waking up, realised that the 'piece' was not yet in and the light still on, so she leapt forth from the top bunk – quicker than ever before – to rectify this error. M sat up in bed with dazed look, mumbling something the while, and drew the curtains, which left D in complete darkness. D could not account for this action but did not probe the matter further as she herself was in a dazed condition. It later transpired that M was doing all these things in her sleep, which was not unusual with M. D leapt back into bed and fell asleep once more only to be roused with loud knockings and ringings on the front door. M sleeping the sleep of the just heard nothing. D not knowing what procedure to adopt let the knocking continue, but one gallant youth journeyed down to see what all the noise was about. It appeared that the 'piece', and her boy, had got lost on the cliffs. D had to have the story related to her in great detail when the female arrived upstairs, thereby losing half a night's sleep.

Although M and D fancied themselves experienced in 'Yo-Hoing', they always felt very inferior when confronted by pop-eyes at the breakfast table who would announce that they were travelling to a hostel that day which M and D hoped to reach three days hence. *Hopeless!* M and D guiltily set off, knowing full well that their necks had not been washed for two days, but resolved to do this duty the following night. (It proved later that this was to be postponed still further.)

The next place of interest to be visited was Boscastle. Although they had not heard much about this place, they were charmed by it. They next asked the way to Tintagel and listened so hard to the directions given that they did not take in what was said to them, although they each believed that the other knew quite well all that was being imparted. This state of affairs reoccurred again and again, and also sign-posts were looked at and not seen.

On their way they decided to have a pot of tea at a CTC and made themselves at home in the dining room. However, they must have been misunderstood, because about ten minutes later they were confronted with roast chicken, potatoes, cabbage, peaches and cream, cheese and biscuits and a pot of tea. Feeling really quite thankful at the sight of this, but inwardly trembling with fear at what the charge would be, they threw caution to the wind and ate it all. They asked for the bill, prepared for a shock, but had reached the stage when whatever shock they received they could keep calm countenances and never register surprise. However, no shock was forthcoming because the bill was only 2/- each. Marvellously cheap for the meal they had had!

They spent the afternoon at Tintagel writing correspondence to fond parents and friends, and afterwards made their way towards King Arthur's castle, with no intention whatsoever of entering same. As they were passing a cottage, an old witch of a woman hopped out and said, 'Where are you going?'

D looked blank, not knowing quite where she was going, but M in an emphatic tone said, 'Just up here', pointing vaguely in the distance.

Not to be put off, however, the woman said, 'It is 6d to go to the castle, and you want the key.'

D still looked blank but M, maintaining her emphatic tone said, 'We are *not* going to the castle,' and marched on. On surveying the castle, M and D wondered why a key was necessary, as the walls were nearly knocked down and the ruins were roofless.

Port Isaac was the next village reached and a lovely tea was enjoyed at the harbour. Much to their horror, they found it was almost dark when they got outside with still about six miles to go. Panic reigned, but M and D struggled courageously on through pitch-black open roads, and negotiated hills as never before. Their speed was so great that they nearly passed the hostel altogether. Only in the nick of time did they espy the YHA sign, and with a sigh of relief they proceeded in.

This was a primitive farmhouse and the dormitory somewhat resembled a cow-shed as the top and bottom of the door opened separately. M and D proceeded to the office to proffer their hostel cards and upon arrival D found that she had left hers in her saddle bag. She returned to retrieve same, and once more proceeded in, only to find that the hostel card was still missing. Great embarrassment for D in front of the warden, but as he was rather half-soaked D was spared ridicule. On returning to the cycle shed, she found the fêted card in her other saddle bag. They were able to see two lighthouses on the horizon from their dormitory. One flashing brilliant red and the other orange. There they met two pop-eyes and one female and chatted well into the night. Great excitement pervaded when they, and the other female, retired to bed. The converted cow-shed housed many unwanted comrades of the animal kingdom, and spiders were dangling from cobwebs at various intervals from the ceiling. M did a spot of furniture removing as her bed was situated near an aperture in the wall which looked as if it might conceal anything. The other female got out of her bed several times to adjust it, but D was too petrified to move and was only conscious of a green light at the rear of her bed. Eventually all was silent and peace reigned, when D, in a weak voice, suggested that an oil lamp might help them through the night. After much argument the other courageous female, together with M descended from their beds. Further commotion was caused by M treading on a soft slithery object the identity of which could only be guessed at. The oil lamp was lit casting weird shadows around the wall, but a peaceful night ensued. M and Ds' resolve to wash their necks was still further postponed owing to the primitive arrangements. However, they were not greatly upset as by this time they had grown quite attached to their grime.

They made their way to breakfast amidst cows, fowl, turkeys, ducks and cats and this was served in a rather haphazard fashion owing to the wife of the warden being the proud mother of a two month old baby, whom they had to continually admire throughout the meal. They were informed that there were three maids but did not set eyes on these, or any of the work they should have done. They were delayed about half-an-hour in admiration of the aforementioned baby and M had to tell a hopeless lie by saying that they would be there next year to perceive his progress.

Eleven o'clock saw them on their way to Port Quin accompanied by a Manchester pop eye who hoped to reach Falmouth that night, but as he did not leave M and D at Padstow until twelve o'clock his chances were rather remote, particularly as he did not seem aware of the route. Although conversation became rather strained whilst crossing about one mile of quick sands to the ferry, M and D were pleased that he was with them as their ferry fees were paid. Great confusion was experienced by D however, in proffering a tip which was refused by the ferryman who told her to give it to his colleague, who also refused it. In Wales it was noticed that people waited for tips, whilst in Cornwall they seemed only too anxious to refuse them. Also, whilst in Wales women were continually trying to promote business; in Cornwall, the reverse was the case.

A marvellous sea was witnessed at Bedruthan Steps and an open-air lunch was enjoyed, consisting of fruit salad, splits and cream. They journeyed on determined this time to reach Wheal Kitty Hostel, St Agnes, in daylight. Newquay was reached, and by this time M and D felt really common cuts especially amidst the 'classy' hotel crowds, so thought it fit to again adopt an accent. This seemed to cause surprise to all the hearers thereof and their faces registered astonishment on hearing such cultured tones emitting from such cuts. Having taken the wrong road, they enquired of a postman the correct route, this time hearing and also comprehending. Great improvement!

On reaching Perranporth, and feeling hungry, they made themselves common once more by consuming plums and pears on the front. Before long, they were rushing up hills in search of the hostel, and remarked how nineteen miles seemed a mere nothing after tea, while ten miles nearly killed them during the rest of the day.

Eventually they arrived at the hostel feeling very hungry, parked their bicycles, and were about to proceed to the front door when M discovered that she had lost her leather case, containing bank books, YHA cards and vouchers, maps and various sundries. Her mind went blank and this caused her to wear a harassed expression for the rest of the evening. However, the warden was a cheery soul and definitely out to promote business, no doubt this was due to the fact that he was the father of ten and although it was nine o'clock he offered them baked beans on toast, which M and D consumed with relish. M showed marked wanderings of the mind, thinking of course, of the lost leather bag, and found herself pouring milk into the teapot instead of hot water. Poor M! At this hostel they had a room to themselves containing two beds. They retired to bed early in order to catch up with themselves in the way of repacking saddle bags, memoirs, ablutions, writing cards etc. None of these things, however were accomplished, as they came to the conclusion that they were too tired and M too harassed over her loss.

Next morning saw them faced with scrambled egg on toast and the proverbial marmalade for which they were swizzed an

amount of 3s.10d for which they were unable to pay. The warden
then suggested to M that she should communicate with the local
police force with regard to the loss of her leather bag, and after
wandering through the village of St Agnes, they came across
the police force digging up potatoes in the garden. This solitary
party seemed ready to accept any suggestions proffered by M
and D but did not offer any himself, and had not heard of any
of the surrounding districts. However, he took countless notes
and turning to M said 'See, you said it contained a Bible did
you not?' M's surprised countenance caused the police force to
realise his error, and he then made the bright suggestion that M
and D should return to the village – about two miles away – to
telephone the Newquay police, despite the fact that he had a
telephone in his own house. (Beyond all hope!)

However, instead of proceeding to the village, they went to
the railway station and there M, with the help of the station
master, (whose whole morning they wasted hanging about in
his private office), communicated with the Newquay police
causing great excitement to the station staff. The result of this
conversation was that M learnt that her bag had been handed
in but that she would have to return to Newquay to retrieve it.
Fated! Again, with the help of the station master they decided
to catch the two o'clock back to Newquay, leaving their bicycles
at St Agnes Station. The 4.40 train was to be taken back from
Newquay to St Agnes, where their bicycles would be placed in
the train by a porter to accompany M and D to St Erth. (This
latter station had to be reached in order for them to catch up
with themselves and arrive at Lelant Youth Hostel that night.)

During the journey to Newquay they were accompanied by

an elderly lady who seemed anxious to make light conversation and, to get herself 'well-in', she proffered two apples each to M and D, and they then had no option but to respond in a cheery manner. Newquay was reached and M and D adjourned to the county police station. They were ushered in and interviewed by the official, M being required to sign her name on the police records. A pleasant two hours were spent there after the visit to the police, and at 4.30 they were at the railway station ready to board the St Agnes train, but felt quite sure that the porter would forget all about their bikes at this latter station. However, the reverse was the case, and the whole station staff (including station master) was posted at various intervals along the platform, to see that all was in order. D with much confusion proffered 6d to one of the porters, who immediately refused it and wandered off leaving D waving the money in mid-air. D was further confused and sank back into the corner seat with scarlet face, while M saw the funny side and was in fits of laughter.

They then settled down to a pleasant comfortable journey with their bicycles following at the rear. When Chacewater was reached and a cry resounded throughout the station of 'All change', both M and D were in the middle of letter writing, and they hastily gathered all belongings and leapt from the train, wondering where on earth to go next. Two porters were hauling out their bicycles, quite regardless of the fact that D's was a new one, but D decided not to proffer any more tips in view of the recent embarrassment. Before they knew where they were going they were following a porter across the railway line, with instructions to 'Hurry up' as an express was due. This made them slower than ever and they only reached the other side in the nick of time. Lucky M and D!

St Erth was eventually reached and M and D evidently created the right impression with the porters, as one offered to accompany them to the youth hostel at Lelant, which was situated, as usual, in the depths of nowhere. They were rushed through field paths, nearly running into cows, their bicycles were hauled over stiles and rushed through farmyards, and although they were breathless and panting, they managed to keep up a cheerful flow of conversation with the aforementioned porter.

The hostel was reached, and despite the fact that they had had tea in Newquay, the Cornish Pasties they were serving for supper looked so inviting that they ordered some at once, and proceeded to bed feeling F.T.B. Rather a wakeful night ensued with M on top and D below, owing to the incessant downpour on the corrugated roof of the dormitory. This downpour continued until eleven o'clock the next morning, when M and D, in desperation, set off first from the hostel, towards St Ives and Land's End.

As they had not had time to catch up with themselves sufficiently to blow up their tyres, they thought it best to have this done at a garage and proceeded onwards light at heart with the resolve to 'Start all over again'. Before long, however, another shower descended, and they rushed into a little wooden hut for a pot of tea. The shower over, they made their way to St Ives, and there drew out of their respective accounts with the post office, sufficient money for their needs.

The journey to Land's End was then commenced and after covering a few miles they entered a house for tea. Here they were welcomed by a motherly soul who was, undoubtedly, glad to see them. They enjoyed a good tea and then proceeded onwards in a gale, but again had to stop for another tea owing to a further shower. [Note: M and D always had a pot of tea when it began to rain.] It might be mentioned that the journey to Land's End was somewhat marred as they were continually tracked by two very fishy looking men, and M and D came to the conclusion that they must be after the money they had only a few hours before taken out of the bank. On account of this M and D stopped the night at Sennen Cove instead of proceeding onwards to Land's End. The landlady of the bungalow where they stayed seemed rather 'fishy' as each time they opened the bedroom door, she appeared to be lurking in the background. Their bedroom at this bungalow was No. 13 but M and D, being cynical about all superstitions, did not let this worry them. In fact, they joked a lot about it, little thinking that very soon they would be laughing on the other side of their faces . . . ignorance was bliss! The landlady proved to be quite amiable and dried their clothes for them which created a better impression with M and D. They here met two Cockney boys and had cheerful conversation until they retired to bed at a fairly early hour. The next morning breakfast was quite half-an-hour late, but M and D put it down to the fact that the previous night the maid had been to a dance and M and D, having been young themselves once, did not make a fuss.

Their bicycles, at this stage of the tour, were beginning to look a bit the worse for wear so D obligingly gave M one of her *gloves*, retaining the other for her own use, and they both set to work on their respective machines. D went gloveless on her way!

The journey to Land's End was re-commenced and on arriving there they were pounced upon by the Coast Guard who seemed most anxious to show them round. This individual

On the rocks!

Which way? A momentous choice!

was most interesting and took their photographs on the last two rocks in England thereby getting himself quite 'well in'.

M and D were greatly impressed by his pleasant manner and flattered by the fact that he thought them Londoners. They decided to tip him 6*d* but on arrival back, he soon put them right on that point and said 'I usually take a shilling each please, and M and D like a couple of simpletons meekly paid up. They later met two other girls who had likewise been swizzed and were most indignant about it.

Penzance was the next port of call and they proceeded onwards looking forward to a really good hefty dinner, feeling that they could go rash over this meal as they had recently withdrawn several pounds from the post office. On arrival at Penzance they journeyed through the town looking for a restaurant, and finding a really nice one, parked their bicycles outside. D, who was carrying nearly all the money they possessed, opened her saddle bag for her purse and with a cry of horror informed M that it was not there. M looked blank and both were speechless for about five minutes unable to believe that it could possibly be true. The only procedure which presented itself before them was to immediately rush back to Land's End by bus in the hope that they would find the fated object. D advanced to a man standing nearby, and with an ashen face, asked when the next bus left for Land's End. It was unfortunate for D that she enquired of this party, as he was a taxi driver and, with an eye for business, he immediately offered to take them there and back for 9/–. Before they knew what they were doing they were rushing along towards Land's End in the taxi with eyes glued to the road, in the hope of seeing the purse, but without realising that they were on a different route to the one which they had previously taken.

When Land's End was reached they fell out of the door, regardless of the driver, and tore along to the unhappy spot, feeling sure that the purse would be reposing on a cliff just waiting to be picked up by them, but such was not the case.... In agonised silence they scoured the cliffs, and, when their efforts were unrewarded, D descended upon every available house in the vicinity enquiring whether a purse had been handed in, but she was met with pitying glances from all and sundry and told that such was not the case. Panic stricken she rushed into the one and only very posh hotel with M endeavouring to make bright remarks following in the rear. Here she was met by a liveried footman who shook his head but offered to fetch the manageress. This dame was grey-haired (dyed carrot) and had a vinegary expression – her eyes pierced straight through them. D, in a state of agitation, timidly asked if her purse had been handed in, quite forgetting to adopt the necessary accent for this type of hotel, but was turned away with caustic remarks and without hope. Poor D!

They then returned to the taxi to find the chauffeur relating to a throng of locals the sad story of the loss, without knowing what was lost. When M and D appeared upon the scene he enquired several times as to what the missing article was but M and D pretended they did not know as they had taken an instant dislike to this piece. However, the crowd soon gathered that it was a purse full of money which had been lost and such remarks as 'what a tragedy', 'so many dishonest people about these days' and 'such a mixed crowd visit Land's End' were distinctly heard by M and D making them more depressed than hitherto. It was then suggested that the Sennen police should be visited and in next to no time M and D were bumping along the road in the aforementioned taxi while the driver, in an effort to promote further business, kept suggesting that they should make a detour in the taxi along the road they had formerly taken, informing them he would do this for 15/–. M emphatically told him that she only possessed 10/– meanwhile slyly passing D a £1 note so that when she paid the 9/– he would not see it reposing in her purse. The suggested detour was abandoned and they proceeded on to the Sennen police.

Arriving at the police station, they waited on the doorstep with baited breath hoping against hope that good news awaited them. They were ushered into a room by a very obliging constable and countless notes were taken, the police offering to go and search the cliffs. However, D assured him that this she had done and so, with a promise that he would communicate with his district offices, and the suggestion that they should get in touch with the Penzance police, they again entered the taxi and were rushed back to Penzance, again with eyes glued to the road, but again on the wrong route. It might here be mentioned that this constable absolutely convinced D, by the time he had finished talking to her, that the purse would no doubt be found in her saddlebag if only she had looked thoroughly and he said he had had many such cases.

Exhaustion had now overcome M and D as no particle of food had been seen since breakfast and it was now 4.30 p.m. They leapt from the taxi and having now to act as exchequer offered the 9/– to the chauffeur. This piece who appeared to be sympathetic (M and D knowing all the time he was only out to promote business) said 'You ought to give me 10/– you know, honestly you should' and M, with an anxious eye on D, not knowing what she was doing nor why she did it thrust a 10/– note into the man's hand. He then proffered his dirty palm and said 'Well, the best of luck miss'. Without enthusiasm and without even looking at him M and D placed their clammy hands in his and hurried of in search of the Penzance police.

They rushed up the main street looking like a couple of fanatics and upon espying a policeman on point duty advanced upon him and enquired the way to the police station. Five minutes later saw them blinding into the borough police station. The sergeant appeared on hearing the commotion outside, to be met by a couple, both wearing terribly harassed expressions, and both nibbling their finger nails. D was in such a state of anxiety that she could hardly explain her mission, and whilst the sergeant was taking notes, M several times had to put D right on various points. D even seemed to forget what her name was, let alone her address. However they both seemed to have made a marked impression on the sergeant and, probably, in view of their helplessness, he conceived the brilliant idea to phone up the St Just police. A long conversation ensued, the outcome of which was that a purse had been found by a gentleman at Land's End, who had left by aeroplane for the Scilly Isles taking the object with him. It was thought that this might be D's. A trunk call was then put through to the hotel at which the gentleman was staying on the Isles of Scilly, and the sergeant was informed that the gentleman was out but would communicate with the police that night. This promised promptitude was, no doubt, due to the fact that the sergeant had made it clear entirely on his own initiative, that the money was badly needed by two girls who could ill afford to lose it. M and D did not suffer any delusions regarding their appearance after this remark!

On leaving, they were asked to call again to hear the result of the finder's conversation that night, the sergeant making it quite clear what his hours of duty were. Now that M and D felt that that which had been lost had been found, and being in a state of starvation, proceeded to an expensive looking restaurant to have a 'bust up', and did not even think of first going into the cloakroom to make themselves respectable. A marvellous meal was enjoyed and they then set off to look for the night's abode, not having anticipated staying in Penzance. They eventually got settled in a very nice CTC establishment, and afterwards once more made their way to the police station. There was no news forthcoming although they felt quite sure that the purse was D's, and M and D were informed 'to be on parade' at the station at 9.30 next morning.

They retired to bed early in order to prepare themselves for the events of the morning, but they were in such a state of excitement that little sleep was had.

Breakfast was shared with a youth who was obviously studying for holy orders, but this precise scholar almost envied M and D their exciting holiday experiences, which were related to him over the table. This party was the unhappy possessor of 'cracking jaws' when he ate, and M and D felt it their bounden duty to keep up a flow of conversation to hide this noise. M was in the middle of explaining a route, thinking she was creating the right impression, when he leapt up from his seat with outstretched hands and with cracking jaws said 'Well, good-bye'. D was convulsed in the background and they both beat a hasty retreat collapsing on the stairs outside.

Ten o'clock saw them once again at the police station. They were well known at this juncture by all the police force, who were focussing on the loss, and were obviously expecting them. Further conversations ensued, in the course of which the chief constable emerged from his private room, and asked if they were the young ladies who had lost the purse. The whole police force stood to attention while M and D answered the questions put to them. It appeared to them that the gentleman in Scilly had phoned through to the police informing them that he would return the purse by the first airship to leave the Scilly Isles for Land's End airport that afternoon. This caused M and D some dismay as they had arranged to spend that night at Kennack Sands, hoping to take the whole day over the journey. However, there was nothing they could do but to arrange to meet the plane at the airport, and thus they set off from the police court, D bearing an official letter from the police to the airport. M and D then enquired as to the time of the bus to the airport, there being only one, and having ascertained this fact wasted the morning wandering round Penzance, confronting policemen who seemed to know them at every turn of the road. They seemed to be known so well that a civilian approached them in the high street and enquired if the purse had been found. M and D were amazed that the public should be aware of the lost property but it later transpired that this man was actually the chief constable in plain clothes. Great embarrassment!

Upon arrival at the bus station they learnt, to their horror,

that they had been misinformed re the bus service and the
vehicle had left half-an-hour before. Absolutely fated! M and
D, once more in the depths of despair, could think of only one
thing and that was to take a taxi to the airport in time to meet
the airship. This time, they chose a very nice cheerful taxi driver
and set off feeling much happier, to collect the cause of all the
trouble. Knowing the route full well by now, having traversed
it three times previously, they arrived at the airport to find that
there was considerable doubt as to whether the airship would
leave the Scilly Isles that day as a heavy mist had descended.
However, this lifted and an hour later (during which M and D
made polite conversation with the chauffeur and got on very well),
the machine was sighted off the coast. D went all trembly about
the knees and clammy about the hands and prepared her speech
for the pilot, begging M the while to accompany her across the
aerodrome for moral support. As soon as the plane touched *terra
firma* they rushed forward, D forgot all her thought-out speech,
and almost snatched the only parcel he was carrying. This was
frantically opened, although addressed to the police, and the
fated object came into view, together with a personal letter to the
chief constable, which M and D, without any qualms, forthwith
perused. Despite the fact that it was now 4.30 p.m., M and D felt
that they must reach Kennack Sands Youth Hostel that night.
Owing to their financial state and after being transported to
the police station once more by the taxi, they entered in a state
of jubilation in order for D to sign the police records, and thus
be on the books for ever and aye! However she did not let this
worry her as she knew that M was already on the records of the
Newquay police. Mild flirtations were then carried on with two

constables who were in the guard room and 5.30 saw them once more on their way.

They decided to concentrate and, in silence, headed towards the hostel. By this means they certainly covered the ground and were about three miles from the hostel when a mist descended upon the Goonhilly Downs over which they were travelling. At this juncture, after not having seen a solitary soul or house for many miles, they espied three decidedly 'fishy looking' men on bicycles making circles round themselves at some cross-roads. M and D should have turned right at these cross-roads, but being in a state of fright, they blinded straight on thinking they could reach the hostel by another route. However, they soon discovered that the road they were taking lead to nowhere, and they were forced to turn back, only to find that two of the men were following them and the mist was quickly thickening. On getting back to the cross-roads the remaining fishy individual was loitering about and M and D were soon aware that the unwanted trio were following in the rear. M kept begging D to look round to see if they were still pursuing them, but D was nearly exhausted and could barely turn the pedals of her bike in the effort to keep up with M who seemed to be endowed with superhuman strength and who was pedalling madly in top gear yards in front. As usual, their Guardian Angels were with them and they arrived at the hostel safe and sound although panic reigned. The warden of the hostel was told of this experience and asked for the particulars of these men. M and D, however, could not supply them.

A good meal was enjoyed with a gorgeous amount of cream and M and D related to the other hostellers their many and varied experiences, and it seemed to be the general opinion that M and D moved in a whirl of excitement and these people considered their holidays very tame. On retiring to bed they were involved in a long discussion with a 'piece', sharing the same bedroom, on 'Spiritualism', etc., which lasted until midnight causing M to spend a somewhat sleepless night.

Next morning it was bright and sunny and they set off for the Lizard, afterwards reaching Helford where a ferry had to be taken. As the ferryman lived on the opposite side of the river, they were instructed to go to the public telephone kiosk and phone him. This seemed an easy matter, but on espying the said kiosk it was found that the door was guarded by a ferocious-looking dog who insisted upon showing his teeth and growling when M and D approached. This caused them to even anticipate cycling up the river and down the other side, a matter of about twenty miles. However, on espying a woman approaching the kiosk, D popped the question, 'Does this dog bite?'

The woman, endeavouring to put M and D at their ease, said in an unconvincing manner – 'Well, I don't think he has ever bitten anyone yet, but I don't like the look of him myself.'

With this she invited M and D down to her cottage to give them some bread with which to appease the appetite of the animal. She also informed them that his name was Bonzo thinking that this might create the right impression with the dog. M and D, equipped with this dainty morsel, approached the kiosk in an airy manner, and M, overcome by bravery, said in a very high-pitched voice, 'Hello, Bonzo!', frantically threw the piece of bread at his tail and dashed madly into the box. D stood helpless and trembling at the bottom of the steps. Having safely reached her haven of refuge,

M prepared to commence negotiations, but on opening her purse found she had no change, so signalling to D, who by now was congratulating herself that she would not have to pass the dog, she made the state of affairs known. D went white at the thought, but pulling herself together, she opened her purse and prepared to approach M but found she had no change either. M, with a little more signalling, made it clear to D that she must procure some at the earliest possible moment, as the dog was, by this time, 'smelling a rat' and his fury was growing. D, only too glad to leave the scene of action for a minute, called on the afore-mentioned woman and changed a *6d* piece, overwhelmed by the cloud that she must return to M. Summoning all her courage and clasping her piece of dry bread, D hurled the tit bit in the direction of the animal's mouth and flung herself on poor M in the telephone box. The ferryman was phoned, but was very curt and extremely annoyed at having to cross the ferry as the tide was low.

The time had now arrived to make an exit from the box and they sheepishly emerged, carrying on a conversation, in honeyed tones with the dog until they were out of sight and all was well! A long walk to the boat followed, during which stiles had to be surmounted and also thousands of steps down to the beach. After about half an hour's delay, the ferryman put in an appearance, but the water was far too shallow for the boat to reach the shore. M and D were asked if they could swim but they replied decisively in the negative. With a sigh the man suddenly sprang at D, and before she knew where she was, she found herself being carried in his arms over fast flowing water, leaving poor M stranded on the shore with two bikes. However, the same procedure was followed with M and the two bikes. The voyage was passed in stony silence,

the ferryman no doubt thinking of the repetition which had to
take place at the other shore. A tip in this case was not refused but
accepted greedily which made M and D feel that it was not enough.

From Helford the journey to Falmouth was very lovely and
M and D, having a definite 'sinking' feeling, made their way
to a restaurant on entering the latter town. They put paid to a
plate of sausage and chips with many etceteras. They found the
hostel in due course and were leapt upon by an elderly 'piece'
who informed them that she was a member of the YHA and that
she had travelled by bus from Plymouth that day. (Some youth
hosteller!) M and D, in very happy spirits, meandered around
Falmouth and were suddenly confronted by a large crowd. In
their curiosity they approached and asked someone what was
going on, thinking that they were in for a bit of excitement.
They were quite ignorant of the political situation, as no paper
had been seen, or even thought of, since the commencement
of their holiday, so their surprise can well be imagined when
they were informed that 'War had been declared' and that
all the Falmouth Territorials had been called up. Their spirits
descended to zero and they decided that they had better return
home immediately. (What for they did not really know.) The
atmosphere of Falmouth seemed tense, and when they returned
to the hostel they were met by the afore-mentioned elderly 'piece'
who was in a great state because she was trying to get in touch
with her people in Hampshire. She informed M and D that 'you
never knew what might happen to elderlies in four days!' She
entered a telephone kiosk and there remained for quite an hour,
but as this was situated outside the Sailors' Home, she felt it was
not seemly for an unaccompanied lady to remain outside this

establishment for long, so being unsuccessful with her call, she
returned to the hostel and spent the night talking about war
which made M and D feel thoroughly depressed. However, a cup
of tea with condensed milk was forthcoming from this 'piece'
and they retired to bed in better spirits, but still determined
to return home on the first train the next morning. While
climbing into the top bunk D dropped a jar of night cream on
to the floor and this was the cause of great commotion the next
morning. A man, renting a flat on the top floor pitched into the
caretaker in connection with the noise that had been going on
all through the night. This reduced the caretaker to tears and she
immediately sent for the chairman. At this juncture the elderly
'piece' informed M and D that she would take all the blame
and they were not to worry – such a thing had never entered
their heads. Everything was put to rights when the chairman
arrived, as he was quite aware of the awkward temperament of
the subject, and said that they were trying to get him removed
from the flat. The elderly 'piece' did all the talking leaving M
and D silent in the background, but it was quite evident that she
enjoyed being in the limelight, if only for ten minutes. At this
point, the political situation was a little less tense and M and
D thought it would serve no useful purpose to return home, so
decided to make their way to Boswinger – the next hostel. As
this was only about sixteen miles from Falmouth, they deemed
it fit to spend the morning in Roseland (St Anthony's).

A pleasant hour was spent on Falmouth Pier before the ferry
boat sailed and they had the opportunity of catching up with
themselves with regard to correspondence home. Tickets were
booked to St Mawes, but on arrival there it was ascertained

that the same boat would convey them to St Anthony's before reaching its ultimate destination, St Gorans, and tickets were thus booked.

Much delay was caused at St Mawes, due to the fact that one of the mates was leisurely and apparently unwillingly touring the harbour in search of a rowing boat, which was ultimately attached to the back of the one M and D were in at present, and the latter were unable to understand the procedure which they thought entirely unnecessary. However, soon after they set off once more, the skipper approached them and in honeyed tones suggested that they may like to proceed to St Gorans for the same price although this latter place was much further on. This again caused M and D much wonderment, but they remained adamant and made it quite clear, in emphatic tones, that it was St Anthony's to which they wished to go, thus putting the man in his place. Eventually, the boat stopped in the middle of the river, the small boat came alongside, and the next thing was that M and D were conscious of their bikes being thrown, in a vicious manner, in the direction of the small rowing boat. The camera meanwhile dangled precariously from the handle bars of one of the bikes, with M and D thinking that this was the end of all their photographs. By this time all of the passengers were focussing on the developments taking place, when suddenly a raucous voice bellowed forth instructions for M and D to take their places in the small boat which was rocking perilously far below. A rope ladder was slung down and M and D were forced, unassisted, to negotiate this. At that point, they realised, only too well, the reason for the persuasion exercised by the skipper that they should journey on to St Gorans. However, they tried to look ignorant of the fact, in the face of the man relegated to the position of oarsmen, and all the onlooking passengers. Before M and D set off in the rowing boat, they were nearly overturned by the swelling of the river caused by the motion of the big boat, and at a very leisurely pace, the oarsman proceeded across to the shore, casting mournful glances in the direction of the ferry boat which was now well on the way to St Gorans – an atmosphere prevailed!

The heat was terrific in Roseland and the colour of the sea beyond description. Here a fruit meal was enjoyed on the banks of the Fal. They did not leave this spot until a late hour, and were thus forced to blind to Boswinger, but found time for a pot of tea at Nancy's Home-made Cake Shop. D, on espying a plateful of Tuttee Frutees immediately made a beast of herself – M did not do so badly either! The 'party' in charge of this shop was too energetic for words. She wore a fringe and wide-legged trousers, the latter looking unusually hopeless as she must have weighed at least fifteen stone. She was polishing spotless and shining floors the whole time but perhaps this was in view of the fifteen stone. M and D, in the course of conversation mentioned that they were bound for Boswinger, but although this 'piece' had lived on the premises all her life, she had never heard of 'Boswinger', which caused M and D much distress. However this latter place was eventually reached and they were welcomed with open arms by the warden and his wife, and an instant liking was obviously taken to them by the family in general.

By this time they were feeling somewhat famished, although only five minutes previously, for some reason or other, they had refused the evening meal. The only thing to do was to purchase some chocolate in the village, and they set off on foot, only to find that the village consisted of two fishermen's' cottages, and no chocolate available – or anything else. Contemplating spending the night in a state of starvation, they proceeded back to the hostel, and were met by the warden who, in a state of agitation, informed them that a Communist and his wife were staying there. This couple were well-known throughout the hostels in Cornwall for promoting heated political arguments, and for this reason he invited them to spend the evening in the farmhouse with the family. M and D's spirits rose in the contemplation of a lively evening! The party consisted of the warden and his wife, together with his elderly mother and father. The elderly mother had a ready flow of conversation, but unfortunately this was of a depressing nature, covering mainly funerals, accidents, WAR, and gas masks. This latter point caused M to spend a sleepless night with Hitler hovering around her. Their hunger was by this time acute, and all depressing conversations were forgotten when the rattling of china from the direction of the scullery was heard and supper announced. M and D felt it their duty at this juncture to make a move towards the hostel, although feeling very loth to do so in view of the plates of food rapidly making their appearance on the table. This they proceeded to do, but happily for M and D, an invitation to supper was forthcoming which was greedily accepted. The warden, who was sitting next to D, noticed her sunburnt arms and without further ado, commenced pouring milk on them. D was very surprised as her arms were not really burning, and was far more intent upon the food, which was rapidly disappearing, due to M, who had fortunately placed herself next to the elderly father, being well looked after in the way of 'eats'. D only had a scanty meal as she was involved in lengthy conversation, and by the time she was ready to eat, everybody else had finished. Poor D!

When the hostel was reached, the Communistic husband and wife were just retiring and M and D were spared any arguments.

On approaching the farmhouse the next morning with a view to settling up, they were met with a friendly 'Good-morning' from the elderly father who was driving cows down the lane, and the elderly mother gave them a bag of apples. Obviously well-in! No charge was made either for the supper or the apples, although M and D felt it incumbent upon them to proffer an amount. Good-byes were said and M and D were offered a cottage on their land in case of war!

Mevagissey was the next place reached, and here M and D could hardly hear themselves speak for the sound of seagulls. Conversation was entered into with an old salt, and once again turned to war and gas masks, and M and D deemed it fit to make a hasty departure, not wanting to hear any more.

Arriving at St Austell, they decided to partake of a meal, and wandered up and down the High Street looking for 'Quantity and Quality combined with Economy'. They hovered around a promising-looking CTC when a voice from within cheerfully said 'Bring your bikes right inside and leave them in the hall'. 'It's roast beef and Yorkshire pudding today'. M and D in their usual obedient manner were soon seated at the table eagerly anticipating Roast Beef, which proved to be very good.

Before leaving the cafe, the proprietor in great detail directed them to Fowey, but needless to say, M and D had to enquire from several other people before the route sunk in. On crossing the Ferry from Fowey to Polruan, the usual tip was proffered to a gentleman who carried their bikes up countless steps. M's was completely ignored, and D's refused leaving them both in a state of embarrassment. It was not until they were walking through the town, and met this gentleman that they discovered their error, and that he was no skipper, but more likely to be the town clerk! They pretended they had not seen him and passed on.

After purchasing some cheap sweets and having plenty of time to spare, they settled on a cliff with a view to writing memoirs, but were soon joined by a four-footed enemy or friend – they were not sure which – and thus deemed it wise to beat a hasty retreat, the while endeavouring to create the right impression with the dog, by throwing him sticky sweets with which they hoped he would be appeased; however, they did not stop to see!

Triggabrowne was reached rather earlier than anticipated and they were definitely 'out' with the warden, because they asked for a 'tea' instead of the usual evening meal. However, as time wore on they seemed to be regarded with more favour. During the tea a wireless Church Service for Peace was in progress, and this depressed them more than ever. Some very interesting people arrived at this hostel, including, the Communists already mentioned, and an American and his wife; also several pop-eyes. The evening wore on quite pleasantly except for the fact that M made a very bad faux pas. On being tackled by the Communist, she said the war news had come as a surprise to her as no newspapers had been read during the holiday. To this he replied 'Yes, that's the trouble with most people when they are on holiday. They divorce themselves from international affairs,' but M by this time had turned off into other channels of conversation, and missed all these remarks. However, D made it her duty to inform M later.

On retiring to bed, the American's wife was chatty and they soon got to know all the details of how she met her husband and she talked on well into the night. The other girls spoke of how they had met their boys, but as this was rather an embarrassing topic for both M and D – having no boys – they feigned sleep until the conversation turned. Next morning they bade farewell to the inmates of the hostel, and arranged to meet the American and his wife at Plymouth Hostel that same night.

Polperro was the first place of interest to be reached, and here the cloud of war seemed to have lifted which put M and D in a very bright mood. However, they were soon leapt upon by a male who seemed very anxious to inform them that he had had his papers and had got to go up the next day. Go up where they did not quite know. His dialect was not very clear and they could not gather half of what he said. On parting from them, he informed them that he was growing a beard to act in a film, and of this he was very proud. M and D arrived at the conclusion that it was not a very difficult job to be a film star!

Dinner was taken at Seaton, with a bright little male piece, who was too full of his own affairs to comprehend anything that M and D said. In fact, three times he was informed that they came from Birmingham, and about five minutes after, he said 'Do you know Birmingham?' Completely without hope!

As Torpoint was reached signs of town life appeared and evil tendencies came to the fore. Vans-full of soldiers were waved to enthusiastically along the road. Imagine M and D's horror when all these soldiers were crossing the car ferry to Plymouth at the same time as they were! M and D decided that it was one thing to wave from a distance, and another to meet people face to face! A lively conversation ensued and they were invited out for the evening, but thought it best to refuse. When Devenport was reached, much business was done with naval officers and captains of the army – not to mention the police force, for whom, by this time, M and D had acquired a great liking and a soft spot.

The approach to the hostel was made in an evil mood owing to traffic and pedestrians and the address – Swarthmore Settlement, Mutley Plain – filled them with depression and conjured up visions of a convict settlement at best! However, this proved to be a most imposing white building upon one of the most select shopping thoroughfares. M and D having parked their bicycles outside, approached the front door and after many knocks and a wait of about ten minutes, a half soaked piece slowly opened the door and stood in silence with a smirk upon her face which was the most putrid and insipid M and D had yet come across. M and D expected to be welcomed in, but the reverse was obviously the opinion of the woman concerned, but after giving them the 'once over' she mumbled something to the effect that they *might* come in. To M and D the word 'might' seemed quite superfluous. Swarthmore Settlement proved to be an educational centre for adults, and as M and D were left to their own devices to find their rooms, they made the tragic mistake of noisily entering the Lecture Hall where a debate was in progress between a gathering of elderly people whom M and D assumed to be the 'elite of Plymouth'. They rushed out in confusion, and after further wanderings found their apartments. Feeling very hungry now, as usual, they decided to adjourn to the nearest restaurant – Goodbody's – which they later discovered was *the* cafe of Plymouth housing the upper ten. Obviously not the place for M and D, but being quite regardless they afterwards had all their meals at the various branches of this concern throughout Plymouth.

Over supper that night they resolved to cycle to Exeter the following day thereby considerably reducing the train fare. They retired to the hostel to prepare for an early night. The spacious entrance hall was furnished with several tables, chairs, settees, etc., and it seemed the general thing to partake of coffee and biscuits which M and D promptly ordered – to be in the fashion; being observed by all the students as they passed to and fro.

Suddenly tumult reigned and a photographer appeared in the doorway – students rushed hither and thither posing for the event, M and D, in an endeavour to look student-like and fit in with the picture, buried themselves in a book, while various excited spinsters delicately draped themselves round the walls in the hope that they were helping to make the picture a huge success. Hopeless! Silence reigned; fixed glances appeared on each face and *flash*! The picture had been taken. Tumult reigned once more. When M and D had the chance they timidly approached the secretary – adopting accents – and enquired what it was all about. He informed them that this photograph would go down in history and if they so desired he would forward them the Annual Report of the Settlement which would also contain the photograph. M and D willingly supplied names and addresses and bade good night to a small intellectual throng who seemed to have made M and D their centre of conversation, popping questions at them regarding their holiday, which M and D answered in a brainy fashion suiting their mood to the company.

They retired to their bedroom, doffed socks, greased faces, and put in curlers, preparatory to their visit to the bathroom for a much needed wash, in happy ignorance of the fact that this fated room could only be approached through the aforementioned entrance hall, which still contained a large number of people, to which M and D had already bade 'good-night'. Great embarrassment was suffered and M and D tried to retrace their steps, but they were spotted at once and had to bravely walk on, followed by glances not quite so admiring as previously. On returning, the hall was almost deserted, except for a few of the staff, and M and D, on account of their increasing popularity, decided to spend another night in this imposing building and intellectual atmosphere, and abandoned their journey to Exeter.

The following morning was spent in the investigation of Plymouth, and when passing some research laboratories, a cheery voice hailed them and they turned round to find the secretary of the Settlement evidently anxious to speak to them. This caused them great surprise as all other Plymouth people were throwing them disgusted glances and turning round to rudely stare. M and D do not know to this day whether it was their astounding beauty or freakish clothes! Police also wore looks of amusement and many 'glad-eyes' were passed.

Inferiority complexes assailed them on entering restaurants amongst the fur-coated citizens, and so, to put matters right, M and D decided it would pay them, and also give them more confidence, if they wore engagement rings, which would also give the people more to stare at as well as provide amusement for M and D. A visit was forthwith made to Woolworths and thenceforth confidence returned in full force!

An interesting afternoon was spent at the Hoe together with

a visit to the Lighthouse, and after tea, by this time becoming somewhat civilised, they entered a cinema and saw (without seeing) and heard (without hearing) a film entitled *Mr Moto Takes a Chance*. They both seemed only conscious of their flashing diamond rings. In due course they made their exit, and as the town was full of the army and the navy, they thought it best to retrace their steps to the Settlement. On entering the entrance hall this time they were welcomed like old friends, and one worthy student (female), went so far as to invite M and D to stay with her if ever they visited Plymouth when the hostel was closed. Well-in! The conversation took a very high-brow turn and M and D endeavoured to sound as intelligent as possible, but actually knowing nothing about their subject, or even what the subject was supposed to be! Upon saying goodbye to this lady, shaking hands with her, both the secretary and manager leapt forth and eagerly grasped M and Ds' hands in a heartfelt hand-shake, making them promise to come back again. Rashly M and D did so – anything to oblige – and afterwards beat a hasty retreat to their bedroom. However, the entrance hall had to be approached once more as they had left a map reposing on the coffee table, and farewells were made all over again.

M and D were very quickly in the realms of dreamland only to be rudely awakened by the entrance of a mother and daughter – from Oxford – who kept up a lively conversation far into the night, regardless of poor M and D. They gathered in the morning that the mother was trying hard to appear as young as her daughter – result – utter failure! However, she created the right impression with M and D as she stated that although they were going home, no doubt they would be very glad to see their fiancés again. (This speech was made with her eyes glued on the third fingers of M and Ds' left hands.) They felt decidedly guilty, gave each other sheepish glances and sickly smiles, meanwhile remaining silent.

On their way to the station they happened to pass a Cook's Travel Bureau, and fearing that perhaps all their snaps would be a complete failure, deemed it fit to enter and collect a few of their Cornwall books, quite overlooking the fact that they would be expected to purchase tickets. D, in an endeavour to cover up the oversight, mumbled something about a Cornish trip shortly to be taken – M was covered in confusion – but the man obviously disbelieved every word she uttered, and after casting suspicious glances at their general holiday appearance, reluctantly handed over a couple of pictureless pamphlets which M and D disposed of in the nearest waste paper basket! The least said the better.

With sinking hearts, thinking of the fifty weeks of toil in front of them, before their next 'Annual', they dragged themselves to the station and sat in silence for about ten minutes. Suddenly D leapt up and announced that she could not bear to eat her Sunday tea without cream, and without further ado rushed forth into the town, leaving M in a state of nervous tension in case D got lost in Plymouth city. It might here be mentioned that M, with great foresight, had purchased her cream during the two hours they had previously spent in the town that morning.

The crowds gathered on the station, porters rushed up and down, people jostled, trains whistled, signals dropped, but still no D. M, by this time nearly frantic, rushed to the station entrance and in the far distance observed a small speck – which might or might not have been D – but in the hope that it was, she excitedly beckoned and the speck began to run. Just as D arrived at the station – entirely unaware of the fact that she was late, the train steamed in and commotion at once commenced between porters and bikes. M rushed up to a stalwart porter who said he would willingly look after their bikes if they would like to look for a good seat. Happily they did so, but just before the train steamed out, D calmly scanned the platform for the porter, with tip in hand, and a sorry sight met her gaze! *The station was completely deserted except for two solitary, dirty-looking bikes*! With one mad rush they leapt from the compartment and themselves lugged the bikes into the guards' van amidst much whistling and shouting from the guard! However, all's well that ends well, and M and D found themselves seated in a comfortable compartment with their bikes following in the rear. On scanning the occupants of the compartment, they found themselves opposite a clergyman, which rather limited their conversation and general modern procedure! He seemed to be taking notes, and M and D presumed that his congregation the next day would be hearing a sermon re 'Modern Youth', and from the looks cast in M and D's direction, they decided that it would not be to Modern Youth's advantage.

To buck themselves up they entered the restaurant car, but were more or less ignored by the waiters – the food was definitely Birminghamish – the atmosphere worse – not a piece of uniform in sight – the passing countryside flat and hopeless – and they decided that *going west* was far superior to *going east*!

Their bikes now stand at rest, having contributed greatly to the most memorable fortnight that M and D had ever spent!

Cotswold Canters

Easter 1940

M and D were focussing on a route for their cycling holiday and the Cotswolds was the only place that entered their heads. After many weekends spent at each other's houses the main outline of the route was fixed, when a severe epidemic of German Measles broke out. D was confident that she would receive a message at any minute stating that M had been attacked; likewise M However although all their friends were laid low with it they managed by some miracle to steer clear.

It was arranged that D should spend Friday night with M in order that they would be able to make a very early start. Conversation in bedroom at about 2 a.m.

M: 'I could eat a 2d block.'

D: 'I could eat a tin of salmon.'

No doubt the above conversation was promoted owing to the fact that the question of food had been uppermost in their minds for the past two or three weeks, as they intended carrying their own food with them, and many wanderings around grocery stores had resulted in them knowing the exact price of salmon, fruit salad, fish paste, sandwich spread, Nestlé's milk, tinned cream, etc.

Seven-thirty a.m. saw them on the road to town – a nice dry morning. Spirits were high when suddenly M discovered that she was minus her lamp. This was rather embarrassing as already fond farewells had been bade and they could see themselves having to go through it all over again. However the omission was soon remedied and they were shortly ensconced on New Street Station waiting for the train to Cheltenham.

The usual embarrassment was suffered over tips, D nearly funking it but after M had commanded her to proffer same, she rushed up to the porter without further ado. M openly admitted that she herself was quite incapable of doing that job. There was much confusion over getting a seat, but in the end M and D were sandwiched in facing each other which was a cause for amusement. The other occupants of the carriage were summed up as usual, these being, a sickly and pallid couple – newly married; a middle-aged and prosperous couple, the woman being very well dressed and looking quite classy, the man henpecked with filthy nails and hands. The remaining two were males with accents. M and D faced this crowd with confidence as Woolworth's engagement rings were flashing on their fingers. As is usual with them, newspapers were proffered by the males and they felt bound to appear interested, and on nearing Cheltenham explicit details were forthcoming as to the direction to be taken. Good-byes were said, but on reaching the road they encountered one of the males again, and the same explicit details were repeated.

D was anxious to purchase some bread and consequently a slowing down at every likely-looking shop was necessary but all to no avail; the outcome was that they decided to focus on M's stale rolls and purchase a new loaf later.

The climb up Birdlip Hill was commenced, the morning being so warm that it was necessary to be constantly discarding apparel. Happily half way up the hill they came across The Air Balloon – a typical country inn – where M brazenly said 'Cider'. That was enough and for 3*d* each they quaffed a huge glassful, helped down by a chocolate crisp which they hoped would prevent any light-headedness. The inn was scrupulously clean and tidy but quite uncalled for apologies were made by the publican's wife for the lack of maids. M and D found it hard to understand why apologies were constantly being made to them for lack of maids. M and D often wondered if they gave the impression that they were used to being waited on hand and foot by servants. The publican himself offered to give them a lift in his car but they explained that they were cycling and bade farewell to the homely couple. Feeling definitely light-headed and giddy they set off on their way.

Their route took them to the top of Birdlip Hill (where they saw the seven counties); through Cranham Woods to Painswick, where they went round the lovely old church, were successful in purchasing a very new loaf, and bought postcards for fond parents. They enquired the direction to Sheepscombe from some local children, who obviously did not know the district in which they lived, and D then approached a woman who proved to be of the 'sneering species'. Despite it all they eventually found their way out of Painswick, being obliged to walk as D was hugging the freshly baked loaf, which was warm, and could not possibly mount her bike. A spot was focussed upon for lunch, with a barn nearby in case it rained, and they commenced to set out their substantial meal which consisted of salmon, rolls and butter, cheese and biscuits, (not to mention condiments) and fruit. M and D were amazed that all this food had come out of their saddlebags, but they definitely felt it was worth while carrying all their own food when they saw the sorry spectacle of two pop-eyes toiling along, unable to purchase food anywhere.

The next part of their journey took them through Miserden and Sapperton. At four o'clock they stopped for light refreshment, in the form of an orange, when unfortunately it began to rain. They donned hoods and capes, and despite the weather, they blinded to Cirencester where they intended spending the night – never for one moment thinking that they would not sail into a place of rest. For five miles they blinded, the only diversion being the sight of a hunt, which looked extremely picturesque and would have been appreciated more in fine weather.

On reaching Cirencester the rain was still pouring down, and after wandering round for about ten minutes, sheltering in shops, etc., they marched up into the back yard of The Swan Inn, but their hopes were immediately dashed when they saw the Proprietor turning away two dripping males, at the same time informing them that Cirencester was absolutely full that night, and that the police station was the only place left to sleep at.

Glances were exchanged between M and D and they were just turning away when the Proprietor beckoned to them and said that, although his wife was out, he thought she would be able to fix them up in their bedroom, they being willing to sleep downstairs. Sighs of relief were uttered and in they marched. They were invited to sit by a blazing fire and D immediately commenced to disrobe all she could, shoes, stockings, etc., despite the fact that the publican was likely to walk in at any moment.

The wife soon made her appearance and M and D looked forward to being shown their room, but they were completely ignored for at least half-an-hour, when suddenly they were descended upon and asked to partake of a cup of· tea in the kitchen. They were treated like old friends, and discovered that the publican and his wife were named Walter and Vi. They weighed Walter up as a bit of a lad but discovered that Vi was equal to him. After tea they were shown to the bedroom which they were to occupy, being informed that the bed was well aired, which set their minds at rest as their mothers had warned them against the dangers of damp beds. This was the only bedroom which had electric light, the bathroom was next door, there was a divan and plenty of mirrors all over the place. M and D were well pleased and patted themselves on the back.

The next thought which entered their heads was to get a good square meal, and they sallied forth to look for a fish and chip saloon. The town was conspicuous by its absence of cafés but eventually they came across a door with a key in it and cafe written above it, and without hesitation they walked in and up the stairs, settling themselves at a table. A buxom matron appeared and informed them that the cafe was closed, but said she would serve them sausage and chips. They also ordered tea and bread and butter and ate a hearty meal, at the same time judging the bill to be at least 2/– each. Imagine their surprise when the total bill for both of them was only 2/–!

Before returning to The Swan they visited the Catholic church for M's benefit the next morning, on the way back purchasing chocolates and cigarettes. They returned post-haste to The Swan, bent on an early night, and had decided difficulty in finding their bedroom, owing to a complete lack of lights and an efficient black-out. This necessitated the striking of a dozen or more matches. However, they *did* find their room, and were forced to place chairs against the door as it did not shut. They leisurely got ready for bed, put hair in curlers, greased faces in a liberal manner, read leaflets which were addressed to Walter, and arranged their clothes around the room. Just preparatory to getting into bed they placed their purses under the pillow, and at this juncture a knock came to the door.

No reply from M and D, and without further ado in walked Vi, pushing the chairs, which had been placed against the door, with her. M and D sat on the bed, open-mouthed and somewhat embarrassed at being found in such a state, while Vi, in a commanding voice, said, 'Do you mind moving to another room with single beds?' at the same time muttering something about a honeymoon couple.

M and D did not see what this had got to do with them, but in their usual weak manner, obeyed. Vi retreated from the room and a man's voice was heard to say, 'It's jolly decent of them.' Vi returned to their room, disposed to linger and inclined to confidences. M and D felt that this interlude was all to the good as it would give the aforementioned male plenty of time to remove his presence from the landing.

They were very astonished to hear that there was another empty room, as they had understood that the inn was full to overflowing, and they arrived at the conclusion that there was something fishy about it. These suspicions were soon confirmed. Several journeys between the bedrooms were necessary, M and D looking utter 'cuts', and Vi hovering in the background. (They expected to see Walter appear on the scene any minute but he was busy in the bar below.) They were presented with one short stump of a candle and when this was lighted there came into view a long narrow cell containing two long narrow beds, one dusty dressing-table, and a moth-eaten wash-stand. However, still determined on an early night they decided to make the best of things, at the same time hoping for a reduction on the bill, in view of the inconvenience caused. A cry of dismay escaped M as she turned back the clothes – one thin sheet and a counterpane in the middle of March. D remarked that she had more on her own bed in the hottest summer and M agreed. They forthwith commenced to dress again, in an endeavour to get warm, but after about five minutes in their respective beds, decided that the only course open to them for a fairly warm night was to sleep together in one bed, utilising all the bed-clothes (two sheets and two counterpanes). They felt like two sardines in a tin, unable to move, and cramp soon set in, accompanied by severe cold. Church bells were ringing all through the night and never had they welcomed morning so much. Vi entered the room at about seven o'clock, without knocking, bringing with her two cups of tea and biscuits – the sign of a guilty conscience.

On the way to church they suddenly remembered that they had forgotten to enquire re trains back to Birmingham on Tuesday. They immediately thought of telephoning to Cheltenham Station, but decided that it was not worth the expense, and went on their way without a care. They returned for breakfast at about ten o'clock, met the honeymoon couple, were thanked by the husband for giving up the room (great embarrassment), and were joined by Walter and a very lackadaisical Vi. They guessed the bill to be 5/– each but received a severe shock when a sum of 15\– was required from them. Walter enquired where they were spending the next night, saying that he did not think that they would get in anywhere, and suggested that he should telephone his friend at the White Hart hotel, Fairford, to ask if he could accommodate them. The result of this was favourable and they sallied forth on their way, after visiting the parish church. (M and D were often amazed, after sight-seeing, to find their bikes were as they left them.)

Cider was partaken at the Hare and Hounds in the middle of the morning, at the very cheap sum of 2d, and they continued their journey along the Fosse Way. Churches were visited at Coln St Dennis, Coln St Roger, and Coln St Aldwyn, three typically Cotswold villages.

They had their dinner just outside Coln St Dennis, on top of a hill, where they were soon joined by a local boy on a bicycle and a very very old man hovering in the background and listening very intently to all that was going on. He was decorated with numerous stripes and medals, the latter being suspended by string and cotton. When the boy left the old man came to the fore and M and D found it extremely difficult to understand his conversation, struggling to conquer a wild impulse to laugh. The gist of his conversation seemed to be the Boer War. When they arrived at the church of Coln St Roger they got involved with the vicar, who showed them round the church in full view of gaping Sunday-school children, whom M and D felt sure thought that they were their new Sunday-school teachers. Their route then took them through Winson, Ablington and Arlington Row, a most exquisite group of cottages. Engagement rings were again flashed here and accents adopted as there were a number of visitors. They looked over the church at Bibury, and saw a picture of Christ which was very remarkable inasmuch as the eyes appeared to open and shut.

After leaving Bibury, Hatherop Castle was passed, and as it seemed somewhat dull, they parked in a most convenient little shelter, just big enough for two, and laid out a grand tea of fruit salad and cream and bread and butter. Were watched with interest by passing motorists, one of whom was so fascinated that he came back especially to wave to them, despite the fact that he was accompanied by one more gentleman and two females. D spotted an elderly man making towards them, obviously inclined to conversation, and warned M not to look up, but he needed no encouragement and was soon giving a discourse on the squire of the village – Sir Thomas Baserley – a bachelor of thirty, who had £50,000 and owned the hall, the whole village and Northleach also. M and D felt he was exactly their type and wished the old man could arrange an introduction.

They cycled on to Fairford and had great difficulty in successfully depositing the tins which had housed the fruit salad and cream but when D became weary of perilously riding single-handed the other hand being engaged in clutching the said tins, they regardlessly threw them on an estate!

On arrival at the White Hart, feeling embarrassed owing to the facetious remarks uttered by Walter over the telephone to the proprietor, they found his wife was already awaiting them, and after she had finished having a violent argument about money with sundry other people in the passage, she briskly asked if they needed a meal . Not knowing whether they did or not they said 'tea and cakes.' When asked whether they would partake of plain or fancy, they sensibly decided on plain, but on viewing the plainness of the plain they asked for fancy. A plate of precisely the same cakes were forthcoming, much muffled laughter ensued, which was further promoted by the entrance of two masculine females, who, with cigarettes dangling from their mouths, frantically rushed to the dartboard. They then furiously played for half-an-hour. These overbearing females made M and D feel small and inferior, and they shuddered to think what humiliation they would have suffered had they not been wearing engagement rings.

At this juncture they were informed that the woman with whom they were going to stay was at church, and they felt that they would be in the hands of a God-fearing soul. It should perhaps be mentioned that the White Hart was too full to accommodate M and D for the night the arrangement being that they should sleep out but have their meals at the hotel. This was all very well, but M and D with a view to economy in view of their previous expensive night had already decided to surreptitiously breakfast in the bedroom!

A maid from the White Hart Inn showed them to the house where they were to stay. This proved to be an ironmonger cum grocer stores and was so dark they had to grope their way through and tried to peer through the dimness to scan the shelves for grapefruit. M seemed to have grapefruit uppermost in her mind the whole time, and D felt that she would not be satisfied until M had a tin of grapefruit in her saddle-bag. However their scrutiny was unrewarded.

The owner of this stores was an elderly motherly soul and

on showing them up to their room – which was large and airy – timidly explained that she did not provide breakfast, but no doubt they had arranged to have it at the inn. M and D silently let this remark pass, inwardly gloating and commenced to return to the cycle shed to collect their food. Carefully trying to hide a loaf of bread, tin of cream, bananas, plates, butter, etc., under their cycling capes, they groped their way back, thankful for the dim light, through the shop up to their room and then came the difficulty of where to hide the food! The bed was considered to be the only safe place and the said food was accordingly placed there. M, prompted by Providence, suggested emptying their saddle bags of clothes and depositing the food there and this they did. It seemed to them a miracle that they had removed it from the bed as on returning from a long walk to Quenington and a tour of Fairford Church (for which they were swizzed 6d for looking at stained glass windows in the half-light) they found, much to their amazement, that a hot water bottle had been placed in the identical spot where the food had reposed only an hour previously! They felt sick when they thought of how the dear old lady would have felt at seeing bread, etc., etc., reposing on her spotless sheets. Luck seemed to be on their side as on escorting them up to their room with a candle, she said she would bring them a cup of tea in the morning. Potato crisps were eaten in bed and they enjoyed the delight of a feather bed and a hot-water bottle.

As the tea had not arrived at 7.30 a.m. they felt it best to dress and so save time for eating their breakfast. This of course could not be cut up and set out until the tea had arrived, but fortunately this put in an appearance just as they were fully dressed – a pot, not just two cups. The lady showed great surprise at their early rise and no doubt expected them to be off in about a quarter of an hour. At the end of about thirty minutes, after having blockaded the door with furniture, so that they would have good warning of any entry they were about to commence their meal feeling decidedly guilty. D experienced great difficulty in opening the Nestlé's milk, but M eventually did the trick with a hair curler. At the end of an hour, M was washing up in the bowl while D was drying with the face towel when footsteps were heard. D, with quick presence of mind said in a loud voice, 'They will be pleased to have our long letters at home – I'm so glad we've written them at last.' The owner of the footsteps, apparently convinced that they were alive and all was well, retraced their way downstairs and after about an hour and a quarter M and D slunk downstairs and were greeted in a decidedly cool way. They felt their secret was common knowledge.

M made her way to the inn prepared for the usual shock re the bill but came rushing back to D, with a summons to beat a hasty retreat as they had been undercharged and it was only 2/9*d* each.

They took the road to Burford via Southrop, intending to replenish their store of food at the former. They chased a baker's cart up and down Burford Hill and eventually succeeded in getting a loaf, and later adjourned to a very first-class cafe for 'morning coffee'. This obviously housed the elite, and engagement rings were once more to the fore and eyed by all, which gave M and D confidence, although they felt that they were being pitied as the general assumption was obviously that their boys were at the war! M and D even felt sorry for themselves!

They took the road to Bourton-on-the-Water via the Windrush

Valley and in a little 'out of the way' general stores cum post office M acquired the much longed for tin of grapefruit! This was earmarked for breakfast the next morning in the bedroom. They had great difficulty in finding a place to settle for lunch but eventually found a lovely spot and had bread, butter, fish-paste, salad spread, fruit salad, cream, cheese and biscuits.

On approaching Bourton nestling in the valley below, the sound of church bells wafted across the air and sounded most romantic. However, the romantic side of the situation quickly vanished when they were confronted by crowds of trippers in their common best, shouting and laughing and reeking of spirits. Although they felt that a hasty retreat was desirable, at the same time they very much wished to see the model village of which they had heard so much about, and accordingly parked their bicycles in a near-by shed, owned they think by the military authorities, paid their 6d and entered. The commonness of the crowd was greatly emphasised, but the village was well worth a visit. As is usual they looked at a great deal which they did not see.

Much to their amazement their bikes were still reposing in the military shed in which they had so glibly been placed, and off they glided through the crowded main street, feeling that all cars parked were departmental cars. They then made for Upper and Lower Slaughter and the neighbouring villages. At this stage they had decided, that the best place to stay the night was Lower Guiting and consequently many people were approached regarding the route to be taken, but none of the directions made any impression on them. The most helpful informant was a very superior thirtyish gentleman who produced maps and took an active interest. Here again they were so busy weighing him up, that the directions fell on stony ground and deaf ears, but they did gather that they had to continue straight on, and with polite expressions of thanks they went on their way. About ten minutes later a marvellous car, driven by the aforementioned gentleman brushed passed them and much waving ensued. They could not weigh this up and wondered if he was going on to book up a room for them. About half an hour later they again perceived the said car parked on a very lonely bit of the road and felt it wise to rush past.

They became aware at this juncture that the light was fading and they did not know how far it was to Lower Guiting. They enquired of a cycling labourer who looked blank and jumped off his bike. After much shouting and pointing they made him understand their needs, he being stone deaf, and he eventually informed them that it was only two miles. Their hopes rose but were doomed to be dashed, when on approaching the only inn in the place, were informed by a half-wit that there was no room anywhere and that they should have booked previously. D retorted and said it was not always convenient to book ahead, especially in these times. She looked blank, wore a remote expression on her face, and shut the door.

After this treatment they felt that the only course open to them was to blind to Winchcombe, seven miles away, and stay with the police, as they had been told that Winchcombe was absolutely full. Uphill, down dale, along open roads, through gates, across fords, in fading light and stony silence; neither of their gears working, evil tendencies well to the fore, they rushed, swearing at all the up-hills but swearing more at the steep and dangerous descent into Winchcombe especially when D's mac fell off her bike causing a great screeching of brakes. By this time M and D were accustomed to things dropping off their cycles as both lamps had on previous occasions divorced themselves from their brackets, and D's bell was constantly rolling fore and aft.

After viewing several inns in Winchcombe, they walked up to one and a drunkard slouched past them, and just as they were going to be attended to, they rushed out feeling that they could not stand a place such as that. All the others looked too expensive and consequently they approached a CTC as though they had never been to one before. No difficulty was experienced in booking a room – contrary to their expectations – and although the proprietress appeared on the surface docile, it later transpired that she had marked business tendencies. Here they were favoured with twin feather beds and once more stealthily negotiated the stairs complete with breakfast. They decided that it would be wise to inform the proprietress that breakfast would not be needed, adding that they seldom had it, but asked for a cup of tea in bed. The business tendencies here cropped up and the woman ticked M off, saying with a piercing look as though she knew everything, 'Have you brought your food with you?'

Embarrassed murmurings followed, the outcome of which was that they *had* to book a bed and breakfast. Their harassed minds turned to the spectacle of their saddle-bags overflowing with food, reposing on their respective beds, and they were sad! The tin of grapefruit was at once scheduled for the next day's dinner. Rather a come-down after the three-course meal they had anticipated!

After hiding the food out of sight, they sallied forth to a fish and chip saloon, the only thing not for sale being fish and chips. Here they catered for the troops, and for 9*d* M and D received two sausages, egg, peas, bread and butter and tea; also the company of H.M. Forces.

After this meal they retraced their steps to the house, and settled down to reading magazines in the dining room, their engagement rings flashing the colours of the spectrum for all eyes to see.

They retired to bed at a reasonable hour and had a very good night. Much embarrassment was suffered the next morning owing to constructional alterations which were being carried on outside! For people who seldom had breakfast, they partook of a hearty meal, which they had with two elderly ladies – obviously evacuees – who were very interested in their tour and seemed anxious for them to visit Tewkesbury. Fortified with bacon, egg etc., they were fully armoured for the shock re the bill; this was very modest 5/– each.

They set forth for Deerhurst, having had a hectic encounter with stray cows *en route*, and here visited the ancient Saxon church, the door of which bore a notice to the effect that visitors should call on the verger for the key. They were just deciding to do the other thing – depart – when fumblings were heard and the door was opened to reveal a man who looked as ancient as the church. There was nothing for it but to go in and listen attentively to all that was told them. He rambled on for about ten minutes suddenly turning on M saying, 'Do you believe God made the world?'

M, startled, said, 'Yes, of course.'

'Where do you reckon he got all the stuff from?' He then went on to ask, 'Have you ever seen an angel?' 'Do you believe that Christ was born of a woman, because I don't?' etc.

A slight argument ensued but they felt it hardly worthwhile to waste their time with him. On pointing out to them a very valuable stained-glass window he remarked, 'Fancy, I could buy a car with that window.'

They did not see the point and after paying 6*d* and signing the visitors' book, they fixed him with a compelling eye of dismissal and sallied forth.

On reaching Tewksbury they visited the Abbey and John Halifax's Lodging House and Mill. They purchased cards and had a coffee. Lunch was eaten on the banks of the River Severn, and the passengers of every cargo boat waved to them. The tin of grapefruit was here happily disposed of, but a catastrophe occurred when D discovered that the diamond from her Woolworths' engagement ring was missing!

They then blinded to Cheltenham Station to ascertain the time of the train back to Birmingham, made themselves respectable, and set off for the town looking decidedly brown amongst the spa anaemics. More cards were purchased, and they entered the Cadena Cafe for a luxurious tea, accompanied by longing looks from two bored husbands, with their made-up wives, who obviously wished to be on the open road.

After tea they rushed in to Woolworths in order to purchase another engagement ring for D to give her confidence on the way home, but there were none she fancied so she went ringless on her way.

The train was boarded after much waiting, and they found themselves opposite an elderly lady and a naval officer – both serious, but before the journey was finished they were both having a hard job to keep straight faces, in view of M and D's conversation. M and D did not feel so light-hearted, but felt bound to keep up a lively conversation in order to dispel the gloom that was rapidly descending on them, as chimney stacks, factories, balloon barrages, sandbags and camouflaged works came into view. However, they overcame their depression and focussed their thoughts on the coming summer holiday – may it be another cycling one. Three cheers for the open road!

Forewarned but Nothing Daunted

September 1941

Indecision reigned with M and D throughout the summer months, due to the fact that they were unable to make up their minds as to which type of holiday to embark upon. So many people had warned them against a hotel holiday due to the food rationing, etc., that they eventually decided that nothing but a cycling holiday would suit them. Scotland was their first objective, but as they only had seven days, common sense came to the fore and they knew that Scotland was out of the question and somewhere nearer to home must be focussed upon. The next best thing appeared to be the Lakes, which, of course, apart from anything else was in a safety zone; a point to be considered! This loomed vaguely at the back of their minds for about three weeks, and half-hearted discussions took place, the drawback being that they would not be making for the coast. Like a bolt from the blue they knew it must be the south coast – a danger zone of the first order!

People from all walks of life, having their interest at heart, did their utmost to persuade M and D to see the folly of making for such a spot at such a time! Even the prime minister, Churchill, only the previous week had spoken of 1 September being the commencement of the season of invasion! The Electric Supply Departmental Staff were convinced that they would be unable to enter such a restricted area, but M and D, adamant to the last, ignored all such warnings and set forth on Friday 29 August, *en route* for something that promised to be enjoyable if somewhat dangerous. Surely one of the most exciting experiences!

The English summer to date had consisted of three weeks of brilliant sunshine, the remainder being cold, wet and gloomy – not a very bright prospect for a cycling holiday. Even this did not deter them, although both their mothers repeatedly asked them if they thought that they were doing the right thing. They were quite prepared to spend the week clothed in cycling capes, mackintosh skirts, and mackintosh hoods.

After serious and lengthy discourses, it was finally decided that gas masks could be dispensed with, although here again warnings came from all sources. Due to the limited space available in their saddle-bags, it was irrevocably decided, at their last meeting, that on no account should gas masks be taken. The time for their departure drew near and Friday afternoon saw them both at their different jobs, working at a frantic pace in order to leave on the dot and be off to Stratford by 6.30 p.m. M, on the point of leaving the BBC, was hauled back to take a telephone message. Cursing this delay she curtly said, 'Hello,' and the next minute realised that anxious D was at the other end. D, that lunch time, had been completely overwhelmed concerning the seriousness of going to the danger zone minus a gas mask. For a solid hour a room full of harassed males had drummed into her that not only was she laying herself open to the danger of being gassed, but there was also the possibility that admission into such an area would be refused by the military authorities. There was also to be taken into consideration that gas exercises might be in progress. Hence the phone call to ascertain M's reactions. First they said 'No, they wouldn't take them,' then they said perhaps they had better. After dillying and dallying for about ten minutes they decided that the cursed objects had better accompany them. For D, this meant a complete upheaval of her neatly packed saddle-bags; a job which had taken quite a week to achieve. M, took one look at her saddle-bags and knew that whatever rearrangements she made, her gas mask could not be housed in either of them, so without hesitation, and in a fury, it was hurled across the garden, and she set off for D's in an evil mood.

On arrival at 4 Finmere Road, evil M confronted equally evil D who was still in the throes of packing, and was horrified when she heard that M, after all, had entirely ignored the arrangement made on the phone, and had arrived *without* her gas mask. D's mother then narrated to M that one of her friends had been amazed when she knew that M and D were contemplating the south coast, as she had heard that activity there had been on a large scale. D's mother, harassed to death, nobly presented M with her own gas mask at the risk of her own life, and saw them off with a heavy heart, warning them to return home immediately should danger confront them.

Off they set in a drizzle of rain, D swinging a 'Shufflebothams of Moseley' paper carrier from her handlebars, a thing never known before, and M swinging from her handle-bars D's mother's gas mask. As they neared Hall Green Church, the rain

increased in intensity and shelter was sought in the churchyard.
This soon passed over, their evil tendencies left them, and they
set off, this time in earnest, for Shottery Hostel. It might here be
mentioned that never before had their bikes been so heavy with
luggage, probably due to the fact that they had been compelled
to take emergency rations, in case of shortage of food, and 2*d*
blocks filled all crevices, not to mention jars of butter, jam, cheese,
salmon and Nestlé's milk!

Another shower descended as they approached Henley.
Hunger set in, and they parked under the bridge to keep dry and
consumed 2*d* blocks. This delayed them for about half-an-hour,
and as they also got lost, darkness enveloped them rapidly before
they reached the hostel, D without a lamp! By the light of M's
they found the village and on espying an obvious youth hosteller
they asked him if they were going in the right direction. He put
them right but warned them that it was a very primitive hostel
so, having had some previous experience of primitive hostels,
they were prepared for the worst.

The worst confronted them on arrival. The warden, a rather
half-soaked individual, was surrounded by evacuated deaf and
dumb children and seemed far too busy with these to take a
very active interest in the hostel. Their dormitory, approached
by half-a-dozen rickety wooden steps, was devoid of all light, air
and comfort. It was in fact just a loft housing wood-lice and other
insects of that type and class. By the light of M's blacked-out
torch they grappled with making their beds which were three
inches from the floor and hard as iron. They then made their way
to the cycle shed to adjust D's carrier which, under the weight
of her saddle-bags had collapsed. The youth they had previously

met, came to the rescue, and they retired to their comfortless loft for the night. On the way up they noted a green light which was undoubtedly giving code messages, whether enemy or friend they knew not. Searchlights flashed across the sky and planes droned overhead but with it all they soon went off to sleep. Well into the night D was awakened by the entry of girls who had been to the Stratford Theatre, and on hearing them mention 'mice' her heart leapt and, stretching out her hand, she removed all food from the floor.

The next morning when all were busy cooking their own breakfasts, M and D felt superior as they had ordered theirs. One or two of the hostellers were surprised when they learnt this as they said that they had understood that no meals were provided. M, who was in possession of all the hostel booking cards for the week, perused the Shottery one and discovered to her horror that breakfast was *not* provided. Only one course was open to them – breakfast in Stratford. Poor M and D.

Faint with hunger and thirst they entered Stratford at 8.30 hoping to find a restaurant open, but alas, the town was dead, and they spent a miserable half-hour rushing round in small circles. During these meanderings D's carrier once more collapsed, and their objective was now to find a cycle repairer, not a restaurant, necessitating a lot more wandering round. However, they eventually found one, left the bike and wandered off to a third rate café, where they breakfasted with the transport people, (lorry drivers, labourers, etc.) eating D's sausage rolls surreptitiously under the table.

Stratford was left at 10 a.m. It was of course necessary now to blind, and this they did until reaching the Red Lion at Long

Compton where they indulged in a glass of sparkling cider! Here the red-faced, loud-voiced publican gave them full details of the route to the Rollright Stones. M focussed successfully but knew that D had not. However, on espying the tremendously steep hill to the Rollright Stones they decided against a visit there, and continued on to Chipping Norton with planes roaring overhead all the time. On arrival there they went in search of milk to drink with their dinner, but being unsuccessful they resorted to cider's little sister (Cydrax) once more. The sun shone brilliantly upon them as they enjoyed their out-of-doors lunch which consisted of Cornish pasties, chocolate and sweets, etc., but they were harassed to death by the presence of sundry wasps which eventually were cornered in one of the Cydrax empty bottles. They would nearly have died a lingering death had it not been for the fact that they had to be released, in order for the bottle to be returned and the 1*d* collected. Lucky wasps!

During the afternoon they had the offer of a lift in an Air Force lorry, but scorned it as they knew that it would lower their prestige as cyclists. A little later on they passed an aerodrome, where the drone of planes was simply terrific. Bombers and fighters were continually taking off and landing, and although large notices read 'No Waiting,' M and D wobbled along on their bikes at snail's pace with eyes uplifted to the heavens, and entirely oblivious of all oncoming traffic. Each of them silently ruminated that all was well at the present time as the planes were English, but their unspoken thoughts were, that upon nearing the coast these would undoubtedly be German.

As they neared Oxford city traffic whizzed by, people were everywhere, and evil tendencies were well to the fore. The obvious and imperative thing was to park their bikes, and after wandering aimlessly up and down the crowded main streets, they were eventually successful, but thought they would never see them again as their two bikes were left reposing on the pavement as there was no further room in the garage. But by this time they had become such an encumbrance that they regardlessly walked off, leaving their saddle-bags to be ransacked by all and sundry.

W.H. Smith's, the booksellers, was visited, where M purchased brown paper and string with which to send home, what she considered, was unwanted luggage. D had no idea of M's intention, and was burying herself in books at the other end of the shop. When M arrived, complete with packing material, D commenced to mentally make a list of what she could return, but unlike M, got no farther and went hampered on her way. The Cadena

Café was entered for tea, but this establishment proved to be already packed, and so they had to focus elsewhere. Their tea consisted of green salad and bread and butter and while this was being devoured they noticed plate upon plate of cream cakes being distributed at various tables. Not having seen a cream cake in Birmingham for months, they immediately made it known that they wished for some. Had they been aware of the price they would have

M and D cycling through Oxford

most certainly have foregone the aforementioned cakes! (5*d*
each – pre-war price 1½*d*.)

Bikes were once more sought, their intention being to make
for the hostel. It was necessary for them to ask the details of
the way to Manchester College – the hostel, and they made a
determined and successful effort to listen, and not only to hear
but inwardly digest what was said to them. Consequently they
reached the hostel in record time where they were met by a very
efficient female with an Oxford accent. The hostel was one of the
Colleges loaned to the YHA for the vacation, and an atmosphere
of learning pervaded the place. This was a very popular hostel and
there seemed to be people, rooms, and beds everywhere. M and D
were shown into a spacious apartment on the ground floor which
housed three overlays reposing on the said floor. After making
their beds they went sight-seeing round the colleges when D made
a *faux pas*. On espying an elderly gentleman approaching and not
being sure where Magdalene College was situated, she enquired
of this gentleman. She very quickly realised that 'Magdalene'
had not been correctly pronounced in the Oxford fashion. A
look of positive horror spread itself over his countenance and he
said. 'Oh, you mean *Maudlin*'. She supposed she did and went
off humiliated on her way.

On returning to the hostel they became friendly with the
two inmates of their room who hailed from Hounslow. The
four of them forthwith commenced to eat in bed and discussed
things in general. At a later hour an elegant figure entered, and
on removing her dress, was observed to be wearing luxurious
lingerie – uncommon to hostellers! M rose at an early hour,
went to Mass, and returned to D who meanwhile had been

preparing breakfast in the bedroom, no meals being provided at the hostel. Sausage rolls were once more devoured, together with bread, butter and jam.

A terrific incline had to be negotiated on leaving Oxford, and the Caravan Cafe was thankfully entered into for cups of tea. This was a shack, such as may be found in the Wild West, and on entering they felt sure that it was. Numerous ranchers were seated around rough wooden tables, and M and D felt that they were the only white women in the backwoods of Texas! In fact, they would not have been surprised had the order 'stick 'em up', been hurled at them. To the accompaniment of prairie music they drank their tea out of mugs at least one-inch thick!

Leaving the backwoods, they cycled towards Childrey and Wantage, devouring chocolate on the roadside, and later consuming ½-pint bottles of rich creamy milk purchased from a neighbouring dairy. Originally this milk was meant to be drunk with their dinner, but due to the heat of the day and M's evil tendencies at having two bottles of milk clanking on her back in the rucksack, they were consumed about three minutes after being purchased.

By this time they had *completely* lost their bearings. Maps were, of course, very useful when one knows one's approximate whereabouts to start with, but when one is completely at a loss and has not even the vaguest idea of where one is, any amount of map-studying was entirely fruitless, as M and D discovered to their dismay. Consequently they were perpetually approaching individuals to ascertain their present position and the direction in which they wished to go. Even then they continued on their way harassed with doubts.

Their road to Lambourn led them through wild, remote,

rolling downland, and they parked for lunch right at the top of Lambourn Hill, where they enjoyed salmon, rolls and butter, cheese and biscuits, chocolate and fruit sweets. Feeling badly in need of a drink, they toured on to Lambourn village, and entered the Red Lion for a pot of tea; also ordering a jug of cold water which they drank like fish. The waitress here – if such she could be called – was either a half-wit or half-soaked, more likely the former. They emerged into the boiling sun feeling much refreshed. D was feeling so full of beans that she knocked her bike straight over into the road, and as the camera was resting on the front of same, they knew for a certainty that from that moment onwards all snaps would be complete failures! Poor M and D. Still being hazy as to their route, D enquired from a man with a dog, the way to Newbury. He seemed very anxious to enter into conversation, and simply could not credit that M and D hailed from Birmingham, as their accent did not in the least resemble the Midland dialect. Good for M and D! Having almost to be rude to get away, they commenced a clear run to Weston Hostel, where they arrived at about five o'clock.

The hostel, which was a farmhouse, was tucked away among trees and proved to be a clean and spacious building inside. The warden, a woman of about forty-five was most attractive and very refined, appearing to have countless young sons and their friends draped around her. Two top bunks were selected by M and D, and while M was washing in the bathroom D made the acquaintance of a female hiker, who clumped into the room in hob-nailed boots, and whom D immediately weighed up to be a 'Know-all'! This decision was later proved to be correct.

As dinner was at seven o'clock they decided to ride to Newbury, and set off saddle-bagless with this intent. On reaching the main road to Newbury, with its constant stream of heavy traffic, depression set in, and they turned their backs on Newbury and returned to the by-lanes, thereafter telling hopeless lies to Know-all who had previously been told of their intended visit. They even went so far as to glibly describe the set-out of the town!

When they returned they entered the common room, which was a really delightful room, Know-all was efficiently whizzing around laying the supper, and made M and D immediately feel young and incapable. They left her in command of the situation and forthwith commenced to read. When supper was served – a scrumptious meal – complications set in! It appeared that a Czech, who knew very little English, had failed to order a meal and this seemed to greatly worry two other men, who also seemed to be in a predicament with regard to their meals. In the end the Czech, who appeared to be overcome with embarrassment, disappeared from the scene of action altogether. The one male produced his own tin of sardines and said that he would be satisfied with those, while the third party, who resembled an unfilleted sole standing on end, and weighed up by M to be a C.O. tucked into a square meal and, in fact, cleared up all the scraps. During this meal M and D, in order not to disgrace themselves by giggling, had to exercise great self-control, but the climax was reached when Know-all, who had charge of all the proceedings up to the present, without warning queried, 'Do you consider the Jews are a race or a religion?' The unfilleted sole looked profound. The other male, who appeared to be frightened of Know-all focussed still harder upon his sardines, while M and D promptly collapsed.

The debate was continued by a few academic remarks from the U.S. followed by an emphatic statement by D saying that the answer was 'race', valiantly backed up by M who had the same ideas, but all opinions were scorned by Know-all and the matter dropped. Two more girls entered – self cookers – who appeared rather live and frivolous and more of M and D's type.

When a move was made towards clearing the table, Know-all once more took complete charge, leaving M and D and the two self-cookers running round in small circles, all vastly amused at the capabilities of efficiency. D, espying a quantity of apples on the table, longingly smelt one; the warden taking pity promptly offered it to her and said that the others could have one. This they did with gusto and later consumed them in bed, D feeling ashamed and guilty at having ever touched the said fruit.

Although it was comparatively early, M and D decided to retire, and before mounting their bunks drew back the black-out to reveal vivid moonlight and countless searchlights endeavouring to pick out enemy planes droning overhead. They quickly fell asleep, but strangely enough they both awoke at midnight – thinking that it was morning – (enemy planes still droning overhead) and discovered that they were still the sole occupants of the dormitory. As the hour of retirement at a YHA is in the neighbourhood of ten o'clock, they felt sure that things were not as they should be, and either the invasion had commenced and they had been overlooked, or alternatively they had slept through a complete twenty-four-hours, and it was the next night! They both descended from their bunks and peered down the landing. Not a sound! Being unable to fathom the mystery, they crept round the house, and when they heard movements they rushed back to their room. The three other females very soon turned up and announced placidly that they had been playing Monopoly.

The Know-all piece then asked if there were any objections to Mother B, the cat, being left in the bedroom all night, as there were quite a lot of mice, which habitually ran over beds, regardless of faces. (On hearing this M and D breathed sighs of relief that they were inhabiting top bunks.) The less fortunate bottom-bunkers eagerly acquiesced and everyone seemed to think that Mother B was essential, so in she came. Know-all made it clear that the animal would sleep at the foot of her bed and keep her feet warm, but Mother B had other interests and when she did not answer to, 'Come here, you pretty creature,' investigations set in. (M and D, watching from the top bunks – were once again grateful that they were so placed.) A penetrating yell then emitted from one of the self-cookers on discovering that Mother B was tucking in to some juicy steak which was reposing on the floor – just over the mouse hole – and which was meant for her breakfast next morning. This was really extremely tragic but M and D saw the funny side (it not being their steak), and shrieked with laughter. The cat was summarily ejected, the girl being ticked off by Know-all who ruminated that the mice would have had the steak if the cat had not. The owner of the remains of the steak then placed the small portion left on a high shelf for safety, and they all settled down for the night. Perpetual and long-continued meows penetrated the corridors – the dismissed Mother B. They were just dozing off once more when movements came from the same corner, and the same girl announced that half a jar of Vaseline had been emptied on to the floor, presumably, this time, by the mice.

The Know-all told her not to worry as it would probably act as a trap for the mice as they would most likely stick in it and die a lingering death. All very well for Know-all at the other end of the room, but not so good for the girl under whose bed these events were happening! D then suddenly remembered that there was food in her saddlebag which was also on the floor, so she leapt from her bunk to remove same to table. (It was discovered the next morning that one corner of a block of chocolate had been nibbled.) Before settling down to sleep the poor girl had to make minute investigations into the condition of her steak and grimly dwelt upon the fact that the best end had gone – wise cat! How she could possibly consider eating what was left, M and D were at a loss to comprehend.

M and D wished to make an early start as they had a big day in front of them, but breakfast did not arrive until 9.15 a.m. M and D were nearly frantic, but became composed and resigned, when they learnt of all the jobs that they were expected to carry out, and they felt it would be well after lunch before they could possibly make a start. Equipped with mop and broom M made her way to the lower quarters, while D ascended to the upper to grapple with numerous quantities of sodden mouse-mauled or cat-chewed newspaper, previously housing the unfortunate steak. 10.15 saw the completion of their various duties – it was a day of evil happenings, as would be seen from the following.

Hungerford had first to be reached; this was managed fairly successfully, but how to get to get out of Hungerford was their first problem. A group of people was approached, but not feeling convinced about their instructions, with profuse thanks they went on their way. On turning a corner out of view of the first group, they approached more people, whose directions were entirely opposite to those laid down by the first. This meant re-passing the first and they slunk back shamefacedly. M still had doubts as to the reliability of the instructions received, so D approached an elderly policeman, who was slightly sarcastic, and seemed bent upon sending them on the main road to Marlborough. With profuse thanks once more they again set of, M still feeling very doubtful. (As an aside, D had just informed M that she had always trusted M implicitly where routes were concerned, but hitherto she had always kept M in complete ignorance of that, as she thought the great responsibility would overburden her. M had been labouring under the delusion in thinking that D was intelligent when she discussed routes with her, and that news came as a bit of a blow.) Fortunately at that juncture another policeman cropped up, and they felt it imperative to make still further enquiries, this time having a feeling of satisfaction.

Happily they wended their way onwards, when suddenly they came upon a despatch rider eating lunch by the roadside. Much waving and smiling ensued and, to their amazement, about twenty minutes later he passed them, shouting as he whizzed by 'Have you a spanner?' Neither of them had the slightest idea what a spanner looked like, so M handed over a bag of tools when he dismounted, and he commenced to knock and bang at his combination. Apparently the result was satisfactory and he then made enquiries as to the route they were taking. M entered into lengthy and complicated explanations, while D, who was in a trance and far away, was suddenly brought to earth by the arrival of the previously mentioned eater of sardines at the youth hostel. A conversation was immediately set up between them, regarding routes, on which subject D was entirely ignorant. After much debating amongst this foursome M and D, left to themselves, wondered where they had been, where they were, where they were going and why?

M and D now wondered if they looked like fifth columnists, as many times they were given entirely wrong routes by people, sometimes the oldest inhabitants, who should have been familiar with the surrounding district. No doubt they felt that they were doing their duty to king and country by misleading such obvious spies! M and D however were too crafty for the likes of these, and continued to make enquiries until they were satisfied that they had been informed correctly.

A military coal cart hovered round them for the main part of their journey to Upavon, and not being content with smiling and waving, they had to throw coal, presumably for luck! The offer of a lift was rejected. A little further on they were overtaken by members of the Tank Corps driving a transport lorry. All this lot dismounted to wait for M and D who were puffing and blowing up a hill. On arrival they exchanged greetings and light conversation! They were offered a lift – again rejected as they felt it would lower their prestige as cyclists.

Faint and weary, lunch was eaten just outside Upavon and very near to Salisbury Plain. Here a heavy bombardment on a nearby aerodrome seemed to be in progress. They distinctly heard bombs dropping, machine guns and gunfire, but were so hungry that they continued to eat until several planes commenced to swoop low. They then made to move, enquiring of some passing children, in a calm manner, (completely false) whether these happenings were usual. The children replied that it was practise but M and D knew in their own minds that such could not be the case, and they felt that the children were labouring under a delusion. Just as well!

The journey across Salisbury Plain was terribly desolate and bleak with nothing but army lorries rushing past and a continual drone of planes overhead. Countless camps were dotted everywhere (much waving) and the war was brought forcibly to their notice. When they reached Amesbury embarrassment ensued at a chemist's shop, as invariably happens with M and D due to their self-consciousness.

Stonehenge was the next place reached, this also being quite grim and desolate, and they did not consider it was worth paying 6d to look at something which was quite obvious from the roadway. The desolate journey was continued until another village was reached where they went in search of a high tea. They parked their bikes outside a place displaying the sign 'Teas' and timidly knocked the door, only to be rudely told that the place was closed and that was that! Ravenously hungry, even more so since they had been told that the place was closed, they courageously approached the one and only village inn which also displayed a sign to the effect that teas were served. Here they were more politely told, that since the place next door had taken over the business of serving teas, they had closed down completely. M and D explained that they had already called at this establishment and had been turned away, and this news was received with astonishment.

Onwards then for another four miles uphill to Heytesbury,

consuming chocolate on the way. Here they met with slightly better luck in the form of bread, butter and cake served in a tin hut by the roadside! They were emphatically informed that nothing could be served with the bread and butter, so being independent, they walked out and fetched their own jam. Later a mass of troops filed in and without asking were served with lashings of salad and eggs. Who wouldn't be a soldier!

The hostel at Sutton Veny was now sought, and they rushed madly along what they thought to be the right road. However, intuition prompted them to enquire from a group of cottagers the whereabouts of the hostel and, as may be expected, they were going in entirely the wrong direction. Back they turned and off they set once more. This hostel was in a very beautiful setting, being situated on a hill, from where the graceful spire of the village church was silhouetted against the rolling Wiltshire Downs. A wooden pavilion, precariously balanced on stilts on the side of the hill, proved to be their abode for the night, while the house was situated right at the top of the hill, which also housed the common room. Beds were straight away made and they set off to explore the village.

Without any hesitation (foreign to M and D), the Bell Inn was entered and two ciders immediately ordered. When asked if they wanted draught cider they were completely stumped and timidly murmured that they wanted it sweet, feeling just like novices. This caused much amusement to the troops and civvies who were in there. On espying one gentleman partaking of Smith's potato crisps, they discussed the question of buying some. He overheard their remarks and offered them his packet. They demurred but he insisted, and informed them that they were the last to be had in the place, adding that he had sandwiches in his car. They reluctantly, but inwardly gloating, accepted them, consumed them with relish and then discovered that the stocks of crisps were by no means at an end. One local, who thought that he was God's gift to women and a big king at darts, showed off shamelessly, but was ignored by both M and D. He wore a jacket, savouring of the county, being slit at each side. Anything more remote from 'county' would have been hard to find. Further troops at this point entered and became conversational. M and D entered wholeheartedly into that and were there for about an hour.

They now felt quite giddy and drunk and made their way, in pitch-darkness, back to the hostel, to a supper of bread and cheese eaten in the common room. They listened to two very elite and intellectual females from Ascot, who gave descriptive narratives of all they had seen and heard during the day, and M and D felt, that they themselves had taken in very little compared with these.

Top bunks were mounted, M sleeping the sleep of the just. D thought that she dreamed that she had a flea on her, but the next morning there was ample evidence that this had not been a dream – in fact, a reality. Breakfast was served to time, and after washing-up they prepared to depart, when D discovered that she had lost her brother's mackintosh cape. She was in a frenzy. Everywhere was ransacked; everybody was accused of being a thief; everyone was eyed with suspicion; all saddle-bags were carefully looked at and all were subjected to close questioning, even the warden. Having doubts about all of them D despondently made her way back to the pavilion, nearly falling over a baby's pram at the entrance, and there, reposing in the pram was the fated cape! A hasty retreat was made.

As they hoped to reach Shaftesbury for lunch they had plenty of time to spare, so they sat on the roadside, smoked cigarettes, consumed chocolate, wrote memoirs, and waved to all passing vehicles. The road to Shaftesbury was full of beautiful views, one of which they photographed. Arriving in Shaftesbury with a sinking feeling they sat down in an elite restaurant to a three course lunch, which consisted of soup, stuffed heart, cauliflower and marrow, and potatoes, followed by plum tart and custard. They tried to buy apples and plums but were told that, in the case of the former, if they had any respect for their stomachs they would not buy them, and in the case of the latter, the woman had just sold the last of 400 lbs.

The moorland road to Cerne Abbas was then taken, but on making enquiries as to where exactly this place was situated, they were met with blank looks and no one had ever heard of it. On negotiating a very quiet bit of road they espied two ladies – county-bred – and asked them if they had any idea where Cerne Abbas was. M and D were amazed to hear the cultured tones which emitted and also amazed to learn that *they* had heard of the place.

The road took than through wild and beautiful country and they stopped for tea in a lonely spot where they had scones, butter, jam, Nestlé's milk, apple juice and cake. The journey was then continued. They were pouring over a map at some cross roads, when a car drew up and a man enquired the way to Sturminster Newton. They put him right, then asked him the way to Cerne Abbas but he put them entirely on the wrong road. Needless to say they had to enquire again at a house at Buckland Newton, and then their steps had to be retraced back the way they had come, up a terrific hill. They were at this stage getting frantic regarding the route to be taken and almost stopped an oncoming car but their courage failed them at the last moment. However, eventually they met a spinster-like lady on a high bike who put them right and said that they would see Cerne Abbas lying in the valley just ahead.

About another five miles were traversed – still no sign of any place in any valley – when suddenly M espied smoke coming from chimneys in the dim distance. To get to this they had to make a rapid descent, dangerous in the extreme, but they were so overjoyed at having discovered this isolated spot, that that was a mere nothing. The hostel had at some time been a workhouse and overlooked the giant which was cut out of the hill opposite. Here there seemed to be numerous families all living under the same roof, and M and D had the feeling that they were butting in. Lots of fat women were meandering about and children of all ages covered the floors and staircase. However, supper was laid and prepared for them, and they were not allowed to do any washing up, due no doubt, to the fact that these people were ashamed of their kitchen arrangements.

They were shown to their room which savoured of a 7/6*d* bed and breakfast establishment, rather than a 1/- a night youth hostel. No bunks, but a double bed which was focussed upon early. No sooner had they settled down for the night when frantic itching set in, and they were obliged to strip themselves and violently scratch, afterwards smothering themselves in talcum powder. Clamminess also set in with M, and this, coupled with the itching kept her awake until the early hours during which time she was fully aware of enemy planes droning overhead.

They happily leapt out of bed early, to find breakfast prepared for them in the same way as supper had been, and they went jobless on their way.

They merrily glided downhill to Dorchester, and after garaging their bikes they had a cup of coffee, withdrew money from the P.O., and entered Timothy Whites to ask for 4711 Tosca which M had endeavoured to get in every town in England through which they had passed. After M's enquiry a calm 'Yes' was the reply and M, not taking it in began to make her exit in the usual manner, when the light dawned and she went into raptures. In her seventh heaven, M marched out with two bottles. A few minutes later D wondered if they had got Coty hand lotion, so in they wandered once more, and once more the answer was 'Yes'. They then mentioned Coty face-powder. 'Yes,' again. (Absolutely unbelievable.)

They had a light lunch at a very nice restaurant where the waitress (quite different from the B'ham waitresses) was genial and friendly and helped them to find their route. Alas, once more they got on the wrong road and decided that maps were no good at all as they never knew where they were to start with. Eventually they arrived at Morton, where to their surprise, they found the little church had been blasted and was in ruins through enemy action. They also saw Lawrence of Arabia's grave in the small cemetery. A conversation was entered into with a lady at a cottage, who told them how she always went into her air raid shelter. Feeling that this person did not realise that they also knew the sound of a whistling bomb, they mentioned that they hailed from Birmingham, but this comment, although meant to stagger, did not seem to make any impression. Before leaving Morton D rushed back to the church, (overcome with some hitherto unknown emotion) and poured money into the box for the re-building of the church. M looked on in staggered astonishment!

The route now seemed to be hopelessly involved, so they enquired of a signalman perched high up in the heavens at a level-crossing, who told them in detail the way to go. They immediately took the wrong turning and after further enquiries managed to set off along the right road!

The scenery was simply beautiful. Thickly wooded on every side with trees meeting overhead and the sun filtering through. The ground was a mass of varying shades of heather which made them feel they wanted to visit Scotland more than ever. This road eventually led them on to the main route for Corfe Castle, and they struggled along midst much other traffic. On espying a likely-looking hotel at Corfe and feeling, as usual, a bit peckish, they parked their bikes in the private grounds, and made to enter. Alas, no response was received to their many and repeated knockings so, leaving their bikes still parked in the said private grounds, they sauntered across the road to another hotel, and had tea to the accompaniment of the Swanage sirens in the distance, and enemy planes overhead at about four o'clock in the afternoon! As M and D had fully expected this sound throughout the holiday, they received it with equanimity, although it threw others into a panic. M and D found that they were viewing people as from another world. After tea they brazenly returned to their bikes, packed their saddle-bags at leisure, pumped up their tyres and calmly made their exit without paying a Penny for garage expenses.

After rattling and shaking along the high road in a rapidly descending coastal mist, D made the awful discovery that her front wheel was hanging on only by a thread, and was about to divorce itself from her bike at any minute. Just as she was about to set to work on it (how utterly hopeless!), a workman approached at the crucial moment and did the necessary, telling them meanwhile of the disastrous accidents that D had so narrowly escaped! He also informed them that he cycled forty-six miles to work every morning!

On entering Swanage they might have been in New St Birmingham, in a November fog, for nothing could be seen at all; the sea, as well as the whole town, was enveloped in a thick sea mist. Evil tendencies came rapidly to the fore, when no one knew where St Vast Road was. Everyone was asked, from Scotch evacuees, resident troops, bus drivers, shop keepers, policemen, tourists, a baker, etc., etc., but each looked blank, and it was only by sheer luck that they stumbled across it.

The hostel was at the top of a steep hill and proved to be as good as any £6.6.0d per week hotel, and run on most business-like and efficient lines. Everything was spotless. They had a bedroom to themselves, there being only one other lady who occupied another room. This was most fortunate as M and D's luggage was spread over every part of the room. The other occupants of the hostel were all very elite, and the meal that was put before them at seven o'clock, was simply colossal. Miss Riley, who ran this hostel, was around about forty, single and an M.A. Even the household duty list was typed. When sitting in the common room after supper, two college graduates entered, looked in the visitors' book, and one said, 'Two people from Birmingham, I see are here. I guess they've got frightful accents. Birmingham people usually have.' As M and D had already been in conversation with them, it was quite obvious that they were not classed as 'Birmingham'. Hot baths were enjoyed, where they dispensed with the cause or causes of their sundry itches. It must here be mentioned that M's teeth suddenly became loose, and she was ready and waiting for them to drop out at any minute.

Breakfast next morning was very tasty. Sausage had predominated during their journeying and it now confronted them again, but it was served in a very delightful manner and suited them very well. One worthy hosteller remarked that they had 'Bread crumbs in battle-dress' for breakfast. Their household duty consisted of peeling spuds.

Having just settled in Swanage, not even having looked round the place owing to the previous night's sea mist, they now rushed to Bournemouth (true to tradition) via Poole ferry. They parked by the way to have an apple and some chocolate amongst the heather, and watched poor pedestrian holiday-makers from the towns making their way to a strip of beach, already over-crowded. They carried with them sorry looking attaché cases housing, without a doubt, dry and uninteresting sandwiches, with perhaps a towel or two for when they paddled. Never were M and D so thankful for their bikes, and they wondered how these poor souls could pass the day on one strip of land, when they found it impossible to pass three minutes on the same strip.

The ferry-boat was just missed and they had to wait about half-an-hour for its return. Needless to say all this time, sea planes were hovering overhead swooping just over their heads. No sooner had D set foot on the ferry-boat, that she was severely reprimanded by the ferryman for having her bike facing the wrong way. What difference this made she never discovered.

On leaving the boat they cycled to Bournemouth in the ever increasing heat which became utterly unbearable on arrival there. This made it necessary for them to immediately garage their bikes, and enter Bobby's Restaurant for a three-course hot lunch! They found themselves at a table, next door to lunatics, who thought it a huge joke to squirt grape-fruit in each other's faces through straws.

After lunch they made their way to the front and commenced to walk along only to feel that they *must* cycle, so back they trooped. M, on the way, purchased a blouse with D's coupons, which she donned in full view of the Bournemouth crowds, much to the anxiety of the assistant, who thought that she would be clapped into jail any minute for accepting loose coupons.

After retrieving their bicycles, they cycled along the front, meandering in and out of the crowds, negotiating intricate barbed wire fencing, upon which D must need scratch herself, the scar of which remains to this day. The heat was simply intense, but as they were mounted, they had the benefit of a slight breeze. Pilots, who were swarming everywhere, were anxious to make their acquaintance, but M and D knew full well that it would mean a life of grave anxiety if they allowed themselves to get fond of one in a machine.

The sorry sight of both piers derelict brought the war forcibly to their notice. Quite suddenly it was decided that they could stand Bournemouth no longer, so they immediately turned tail and made for Poole; once more buying rolls, etc., for tea. As usual the wrong route was taken, but they were put right by an elderly gentleman, and went on their way looking forward to having a lengthy and luscious meal, together with a 'paddle' on the other side of the ferry, being completely unaware of the time, although they both wore watches.

Whilst waiting for the boat they chanced to look at the time, and in a frenzy discovered that they would barely have time to get back to Swanage for dinner, let alone indulge in a tea and a 'paddle'. However, D adamant to the last, felt that she could not go on without something to eat, and they parked by the wayside, rapidly negotiating rolls, butter and jam, and nearly choking. At this point M and D became suddenly conscious of their tanned countenances amidst the 'pale-faces', one in particular – a man of yellow hue, who was later encountered at the hostel, and from then was known as Pale-face.

It was lucky for them that the homeward journey was mostly downhill, and they sped like the wind, arriving back just in time for another scrumptious meal which they consumed with relish. The hostel gang was still very elite, M and D being the only girls. There was one very bright male specimen, who seemed to be greatly amused by M and D, roaring with laughter every time they made a remark. They later related some of their adventures in the common room, and he said they sounded too filmstar-like to be true!

After supper the station was visited, in order to ascertain if there were any trains back on Sunday, but this 'joint' was closed. They then meandered to the front, found a seat and sat in the moonlight. Very soon they were joined by two young boys of about seventeen from the hostel, with whom they had made a great hit. They were so difficult to get rid of that M and D wondered if these boys were under the impression that they were sweet seventeen too! Eventually they made their way back to the hostel and to bed, poor M lying awake most of the night listening to muffled thuds and explosions, which may or may not have been the enemy at work.

Breakfast again was just lovely and M and D were well in with the crowd. The warden mentioned that she thought they must be very popular as they had had such a lot of correspondence. A visit to Lulworth was casually mentioned by M and D, and this was immediately taken up and pursued by the two young boys previously mentioned, who mapped them out a route, and with profound expressions drew every detail. An hour of this made M and D determined that Lulworth would be the last place they would visit on this holiday. Their household duty was once more scraping the spuds, the number having greatly increased, so M and D decided that they were peeling spuds for the family too.

They messed about all morning, going into chemists' shops asking for Coty Talc and Kirbigrips, visiting the station (where they ascertained the times of trains and price of tickets, finding that they could stay another night in Swanage instead of going to Weymouth as previously intended), and meeting the two young boys again who appeared to be following them. M and D hopefully nodded and made to pass on, but the persistent youths had other ideas, and far from letting them proceed alone on their way, they made enquiries as to their homeward journey. M and D were soon once more involved with detailed maps and drawings of their journey across London, necessary as they had to get from Waterloo to Euston.

Later in the morning D announced that her hair was very clammy so she made an appointment at a hairdressers for that evening. M decided to go clammy on her way!

As the weather was so beautiful they decided to walk to Tilly Whim, have their picnic lunch there, and return to the hostel in time for the evening meal. Food purchases were made, including two luscious-looking cream cakes, which cost 6d each, which later they discovered, much to their disappointment, were creamed-crab. Hopeless!

Much barbed wire had to be negotiated *en route*, and at one point a loud 'Halt' resounded and a severe looking sentry approached with fixed bayonet. They felt convinced that their last hour had come and that they were about to die. However , they assumed a look of utmost innocence and unconcern, and were soon discussing a suitable route with the same sentry, at the conclusion of which he clicked his heels, right about turned and marched away in a truly soldiery manner. They then commenced their hike on the revised route.

As they were swinging along coatless, hatless, and full of the joy of living, they encountered 'elderly', coated, hatted, and encumbered with umbrellas, macintoshes, and attaché cases. M and D wondered if they would ever get like that.

They arrived at their parking spot by twelve o'clock and commenced to eat their lunch. It was no uncommon thing for M and D to eat at unearthly hours as they could not sit and do nothing. By 2 p.m. they felt that it should be 6 p.m. They wandered aimlessly on the downs with the mist rapidly falling. Saw two elderly spinsters, who were rushing along at a rapid pace in case they got lost in the mist on the downs – unprotected! M and D, not caring whether or not they were left on the downs in the mist unprotected, still sauntered along, little realising their danger.

On arrival back at Swanage, they made for the cabin tea-rooms and had bread and butter, cake and some tea. As it was now very misty and cold, they proceeded to a shelter from where they guiltily viewed the approach of Miss Riley, the warden. As hostellers are expected to either cycle or walk all day, Miss Riley must surely have wondered what they were doing in a shelter, reading, in the middle of the afternoon! As they did not raise their eyes from their books, they do not know to this day whether her countenance registered surprise, disgust or displeasure.

As five o'clock approached – the hour at which the hostel again opened – and for which M and D had longed all day, – they proceeded back to St Vast's Road, and then D set off for her hair appointment. Meanwhile M made her way to the church to ascertain the time of Mass on Sunday. They met again at supper, D entering late and looking glamorous at the front, but sadly dripping at the back, having had to emerge from the dryer whilst still wet. Poor D! She made apologies to the warden for being late, but this lady was very nice, and said that D's hair looked extremely smart (front view only observed – D made a backward exit after that remark).

At night they read books in the common room being the only girls. Bed was sought early and supper consumed in same. They had previously mentioned to the man who was amused by them, (he was staying four nights at Swanage), that they frequently ate meals in bed and this caused even greater amusement. Just before going to sleep, they both decided that Lulworth must be focussed upon next day, and regretted they had destroyed the detailed routes with which they had been presented. However, they both lay awake half the night listening to a deluge of rain, which was still continuing when they arose, so instead of going to Lulworth, they mooched about all day. This rain made them realise how lucky they'd been up to the present.

At breakfast, at which a Cockney lady and her husband, occupying a Caravan in the garden, made a first appearance, M and D's key-note was optimism re the weather, although in their respective heart of hearts they knew this was fruitless, as did the other occupants of the room who were confirmed pessimists. They once more had the job of peeling potatoes, but the Cockney lady lent a willing hand as also did the amused male. The Cockney husband made droll remarks in the background.

After the completion of this task, a journey was made to the station to buy tickets, but M discovered that she had left her money at the hostel, so only D was able to purchase hers. They were ticked off by the booking clerk who said (when they kept shooting questions at him) 'I'll deal with one thing at a time'. On leaving the station they once more encountered the two youths of seventeen, had a profound conversation for the second time re the route across London, also learning that these youths intended returning home that day in order to settle down in readiness for business on Monday. Hopeless! Unlike M and D who always left the homeward journey until the very last minute, and usually rushed straight from the office on to bikes at the beginning of the holiday, and from saddles to office chairs at the conclusion!

As the rain continued a shelter was sought, after a tour of the book-shops had been conducted. Here a most depressing conversation was overheard between two women who talked of

nothing but bomb damage, air-raids, fatal injuries and prospects
of 'things to come'. M and D smoked furiously to maintain their
morale! After wandering all round in search of a three-course
meal, they partook of bread, butter, cakes and tea in a cold shop
which closed at 1 p.m. They had to go to an ice-cream parlour
and had hot chocolate and biscuits to warm themselves up.

At 2 p.m. they were standing in a queue, consisting mainly of
noisy boys eating raw carrots waiting to see *So Ends Our Night*.
This proved to be very tragic and they both had a good cry. It
might here be mentioned that the only two picture houses in
Swanage adjoin each other, and while standing in the queue,
they observed the amused popeye (who they hope didn't observe
them) entering the cinema next door. To go to the pictures was
a most 'unhostellish' thing to do!

They arrived back at the hostel to collect the money for
M's railway ticket, and then made their way to the station
where M was overcharged for her bike. M was too terrified to
query this, but D, unlike her usual self, up and spoke and the
mistake was remedied.

After returning to the hostel for dinner, they made their way
to the dormitory, which they considered to be entirely their own,
despite the presence of four other beds. They were then joined by
two elite female intruders, but in a convincing and determined
manner M and D made it clear that there was another empty
dormitory next door which perhaps they might like to occupy.
They were informed that Miss Riley had explicitly told the
newcomers that they were to share the room already in use, but
M and D waived this instruction and remained adamant.

At dinner they were very vague as to their movements that

day; likewise the popeye whom they had seen in the cinema queue. His vagueness, no doubt, was due to the fact that he had spent the day in a most 'unhostellish' manner, as had also M and D. Later that evening they had a session with Miss Riley regarding their proposed early start next morning, and broached the subject of a packet lunch with timidity; also mentioning, if it would be convenient for them to perform their hostel duty for the next day that same night. This proved to be spuds again, but the whole hostel came to their aid, and soon the job was done. They invaded Miss Riley's sanctuary again in search of postcards of the hostel, whereupon she waxed confidential, and said that she used to be a pacifist but now she was not. She had a friend in B' ham who had taken a second degree at Oxford, and said that she hoped M and D would come again soon, not only for a few days, but for a lengthy stay. Well in! Before retiring they sauntered along the prom, passing the popeye whom they pretended not to see, but, when meeting him again later, he insisted on accompanying them back.

Having procured a loaf earlier in the day in case of hunger on the homeward journey, they sneaked butter to spread on it, having seen other hostellers doing likewise, and added some packet cheese which D had carried in her saddle-bag throughout the holiday!

They took these sandwiches up to their room, fully intending to pack them in their saddle-bags, decided that they were hungry and consumed them there and then. Parched with thirst after the cheese, they surreptitiously made their way, in the depth of the night, down to the kitchen, clad only in night clothes and guided by the dim light of a dying torch. They frantically gulped water, laughing hysterically meanwhile, when suddenly they heard footsteps and the cups, which were half full of water, were slung on to their hooks on the dresser, while M and D raced from the scene of action to collapse at the foot of the previously mentioned popeye who thought, with reason, that they had gone completely mad! Poor M was awake half the night, not knowing whether it was dawn or moonlight, doubtless due to the cheese, and eventually got up at 6.30 a.m. and went to church. On arrival back, to her astonishment, she found D fully dressed, M usually having to wake D. They rushed madly round Swanage before breakfast, taking last-minute photographs as the sun was shining. Toured back to breakfast and asked the popeye if he would take a photograph of them. They were in fits!

The time came for saying good-bye. Miss Riley was nearly in tears – so were M and D. Loth to leave the sea they decided on a last ride along the prom, where they wished the popeye and the caravan couple good-bye twice again. Sadly they boarded the train to Wareham, where they had to change for the London Express, passing Southampton where depressing bomb damage met their eyes. On this train, they felt sure they had been weighed up as journalists, as they were completing memoir notes!

Having two hours to spare on arriving at Waterloo, they decided to tour London, viewing St Paul's and riding along the Embankment where they took a photograph of the Thames & Westminster Bridge, and felt that the law would be upon them any moment. In fact they trembled as they replaced the camera in its case, hoping it resembled a gas-mask. Many detours had to be made due to bomb damage, and riding over badly repaired roads. M's lamp divorced itself from its bracket and was thrown across the road, to be retrieved by an elite air-force officer.

This delayed them many minutes and they suddenly realised that they had very little time in which to catch their connection at Euston. Agitation set in! They madly rushed into a likely looking station, only to find that it was not Euston, and they still had a good ride in front of them. They discovered afterwards that it was King's Cross.

With scarcely a second to spare, they threw their bikes into the guard's van, and fell into a carriage, feeling desperately hungry, with only a couple of apples between them and starvation. They greedily munched these, together with a few sorry looking butterscotches which D had also carried round for a considerable time. A woman opposite them provided the only interest – weighed up at first to be like a cod-fish, secondly a waxwork, thirdly a Pierrot and lastly a clown. As her head perpetually rested upon the shoulder of her soldier husband and her eyes were continually closed, they were able to focus to their hearts content!

With the usual evil tendencies they parted at Court Road, Sparkhill, none the worse for their war-time holiday, and still *undaunted*.

M and D, location unknown

In 1942 Margaret married Mr Clive Shattock. They had three daughters to whom they passed on their love of rambling and the countryside.

The next set of memoirs was written by Anne – the middle daughter – describing a youth hostelling trip, made with her mother in 1966, when she was fifteen years old. Why on earth they chose to go in November she cannot recall!

M and A setting off

Forest Frolics

31 October to 3 November 1966

After frantic preparations over days, not really knowing their mode of transport until the last minute, they eventually sallied forth at 9.40 a.m., after having their last photo taken, and bidding a fond farewell to Daddy and Freckles, telling the later that they would not be long.

Determined to be early they arrived at Droitwich, two and a half hours before their train left. To help pass the time they had a coffee and paid a visit to the Catholic church to pray for a safe journey. They arrived at the station at 1.15 p.m. Feeling a bit embarrassed at being so early, in a loud voice for the benefit of all, they blamed their watches and settled down patiently on the station, munching their grub and writing these memoirs. At the very outset, a tragic mistake was made over their tickets. Mummy went hot thinking that she would have to fork out a further 34s, but *Deo gratis*, this proved not to be the case. The fault lay with the ticket officer who obviously did not know his job; his staff were no better.

As they had plenty of time to think (for once), Anne's fertile brain thought up the possibility that Chepstow hostel might be filled with a school party, and from that moment onwards they were not really at peace as they did not know where they were going to lay their heads for the night. At the thought of this dire dilemma, Anne's eyebrow started twitching. She must have had a very observant eyebrow because five minutes later they were calmly told that they were going to Hereford instead of Gloucester Central. However the mistake was soon rectified.

Feeling dismal they wandered into the general waiting room and spotted a button that said, 'press for heat'. Mummy obeyed and a fire sprung into life. On hearing a porter approaching, they felt guilty at wasting public money, and Anne, with great presence of mind, attempted to switch it off, whereupon it backfired and blew up. They immediately left the waiting room looking innocent because the fire was still on.

Fortunately the train glided in and they were very pleased when the guard slung the bicycles on board. They were worried about the change at Gloucester, but were treated like royalty, bikes handed out, lift fetched, and conversation provided. The heated train was waiting for them and they sat in state while three porters, none of whom were tipped, took care of their bicycles.

Darkness fell as they approached Chepstow and they felt sure that they would not find the church, let alone the hostel. By their usual good fortune they were accompanied all the way by two girls who lived in the district. At the time of writing, they had no idea where the hostel was, except that it was perched on high ground as they had to climb a mountain to get to it. All would be revealed in the light of dawn they hoped.

The meals were very good and they were given the task of washing up as they would be away before breakfast in the morning to go to mass. They met some very interesting people including two teenage boys and an older man with a young boy. Although a lot of time was spent in thinking, they could not find out the relationship between the latter. It was all rather puzzling.

Anne did not have a good night owing to a girl nicknamed 'Sniffer'. As her name suggests she did not appear to possess a handkerchief and therefore had no choice but to sniff. As she had a very bad cold this became rather revolting, but Anne did not particularly want to scramble out of her bunk, wake her sleeping partner, and proffer a handkerchief; as this good deed might not have been taken in the right way.

The next morning they set off without breakfast, and made their way to the church. Not wanting to lose their bikes they carefully padlocked them with their new padlocks to the church railing. They heard Mass and were rather annoyed when they were completely ignored as the collection plate was passed around; however they soon rectified this mistake and placed their humble offerings in it with a great deal of satisfaction.

They left mass and Anne unlocked her bike with great ease. Unfortunately mummy's padlock was better than either of them had anticipated, as it would not open. Mummy checked the combination twice and tried again, still without success. As the congregation were very amused about their plight, mummy marched around the other side of the railings, trying to wear a dignified expression on her face, took hold of one half of the padlock, instructed Anne to do the same, and both pulled. Nothing happened! By this time the priest had appeared, and was obviously very worried about the fate of his precious railings. This was not helped when he caught sight of a garage hand, hurrying to the scene, armed with a large hacksaw. He examined the lock and to their embarrassment, the combination fell apart in his capable hands. He was tipped 2s and mummy and Anne hastily retreated to recover their hurt pride.

Anne, true to form, lost her gloves, so a tour of the town had to be made in order to purchase a new pair. This also entailed a visit to the public conveniences. Mummy left the door open for Anne who was left to prop up the bikes. An interfering busybody calmly shut it. Anne eventually gained entrance by proffering another penny.

They at last started their journey and made their way up hill and down dale in the face of a biting wind. As their intentions were good they bought a pile of food, but unfortunately never got around to eating it.

On arrival at Tintern they scanned the abbey, and dived into The Anchor for hot coffee, ham rolls and a little warmth. They reluctantly emerged, purchased a few postcards, and disappeared into the 'George' to write them by a fire. This necessitated buying hot soup and rolls, which were proffered to them on their laps, while the elite were ushered through to the dining room beyond. They felt like beggars!

They intended to make for Bigs Weir but as usual took the wrong turning at Brocks Weir (can't read). They commenced a climb of 900 feet to St Briavels at 3.30 p.m. The wind was piercing and snow was in the air so they entered a shop in order to find a cup of tea. Their greed overcame them and they ended up purchasing two frozen fresh cream éclairs and two lemon ice-lollies. They were given the address of Mrs Berrow and knocked on her door to find out if she could give them tea. Immediately a large Alsatian rushed out and timidly attacked them. They were hastily ushered in and made comfortable by the side of a nice electric fire. A coal fire however soon replaced this. After having tea they were introduced to an extremely hairy guinea pig which resembled a Pekinese. At 5 p.m. they arrived at the castle, and met the two teenage boys that were at Chepstow. They had walked there and had arrived before Mummy and Anne who were obviously on bikes! The castle was very gloomy and had an evil atmosphere. This was not helped by the fact that it faced a graveyard.

St Brievels YHA

They signed in and were delivered a long lecture about the officials of the YHA by a very queer warden. They were directed to dorm three which they discovered used to be a prison. Mummy took an instant dislike to it and felt very uneasy.

The prison opened from the guard chambers through a narrow

doorway and a small passage. The door was of great strength with large hasps and staples. There was a small circular opening in it through which food was passed to the prisoners and an eye kept on their behaviour. The windows were narrow and secured with iron bars, while stone steps led to a stone seat in a recess. Lonely prisoners had passed their time by scratching messages in the stone. Typical examples were:

ROBIN·BELCHER·THEE·DAY·WILL·COME·THAT·THOU·SHALT· ANSWER·FOR·IT·FOR·THOU·HAST·SWORN·AGAINST·ME·1671

MY·GLAS·IS·ROON·TIS·TIME·T·WAS·GONE·FOR·I·HAVE· LIVED·A·GREAT·SPACE·AND·I·AM·WEARY·OF·THE·PLACE

They made up their beds and had their dinner in the member's kitchen. Here they met the warden's wife and their little girl. The little girl was very thin and white and screamed a lot. This made them very uneasy and as they were the only 'girls' they did not feel very comfortable. They retired to the common room where a brownie meeting was in progress. They were glad of the company and had a long chat to 'Brown Owl'.

After the brownies left the two boys appeared. They came from the Potteries and were interested in forestry and geology. Both Mummy and Anne were glad of their moral support. As bedtime drew near they became very uneasy and decided to change dormitories. They sought out the warden's wife who told them that they were mad. Ignoring this they moved out of the prison into the hangman's room, although they did not know this at the time.

Anne had a fairly good night except for hearing tapping on the prison door. Mummy spent most of the night praying for the dead, especially as it was All Souls Night in a state of high anxiety and fear. She too heard noises coming from the prison. As there was nobody about they were petrified but eventually got to sleep.

Brievels church and castle by D. J. Rice 1965

The next morning they were told that they had nearly been thrown out and their money refunded because they had been so hysterical. The warden's wife also told them that one night she had had thirty boys in hysterics and one girl had walked out at 3.30 a.m. because she could not stay there any longer.

After bidding farewell to the two boys they hurried out of the castle, glad to be out of the evil place. They could not understand why anyone would want to live there.

Their next hostel was Welsh Bicknor and they sincerely hoped that it would be better than St Briavels. They had wondered whether to return home that day in view of Daddy's dire warnings of icy roads, etc., but the next day was really quite pleasant and so they decided to proceed and return by train from Hereford. Before actually leaving St Briavels they went around the church and then set off for Symonds Yat.

The country was very beautiful, and after descending a hill, 1:5, with fear and trepidation, they arrived at Goodrich at about dinnertime with only three miles to go to the hostel. After making friends with a person driving a pony and trap they eventually discovered that he was a she. They had wondered why he was wearing a skirt! In order to pass the time and to get warm, they called at a cafe for hot soup and cheese and biscuits. Unfortunately the room they were put in was actually far colder than outside, and they left feeling like icicles!

Two-thirty p.m. found them ensconced in a telephone kiosk on the road to Welsh Bicknor, at the top of Coppett Hill, in order to get warm. Prior to this they had tried to gain access to a house marked 'for sale', but having cautiously crept up the drive, they found that the house was occupied and so they returned to *their* kiosk. They were so fed up and tired of standing, that they tried to rest on the floor of the phone box, each sitting on a phone directory. Once they were bedded down it was extremely difficult to rise. Eventually they both stood up, and after singing a few rounds, they consumed a Cornish pasty that had accompanied them all the way from Chepstow.

At about 3.30 p.m. a very nice lady approached, knocked on the phone box and timidly asked them if she could use the

phone, telling them that she would not be long. They very
condescendingly allowed her to enter. Overcome with gratitude
she invited them to her house for a warm and a lovely cup of
tea. They wallowed in this luxury and during the conversation
learnt that Courtfield, the home of the Vaughan family, was
now owned by the Mill Hill fathers and was just down the
road on the way to the hostel. They left about 4.15 p.m. and
called into Courtfield, went to see the grotto in the grounds,
and tried to gain entrance to the church. At their first attempt
they found themselves in the crypt but soon discovered their
mistake, and eventually managed to gain entrance.

At 4.45 p.m. they arrived at the hostel which they expected
to find locked and barred (owing to St Briavels), however the
door was wide open and had a welcoming light inside. After
visiting three donkeys, which belonged to the warden's two
daughters, they were invited in and showed their dormitory
Cedar. Everywhere was spotless, comfortable, and warm. The
wardens, besides owning three donkeys, also possessed two
dogs, ten hens, and about six cats. Anne soon arranged to be
up at 7 a.m. the next morning to help muck the donkeys out.

There were only five other people there; the young man
and the boy previously met at Chepstow, and three girls aged
seventeen from Birmingham, who were working for the Duke
of Edinburgh Gold Award. In the dorm the conversation got
around to St Briavels, and it transpired that they had stayed
there two nights previously, that they too heard the knocking,
and that they too had been terrified. This left all of them in
a complete state of shock as they knew then that they had not
imagined it.

They had a good night and after Anne had mucked out the
donkeys, and they had participated in breakfast, they set off up
the steep stony track that led from the hostel. Soon they were
once more pedalling along the lane. They waved goodbye to *their*
telephone box and continued down the steep hill.

They eventually joined the main Hereford road and pedalled
furiously, as they had to catch the 1.30 p.m. train, and they still
had 14 miles to go. Seven miles further on they stopped at a
little pub in order to refresh themselves. Here they were told
that it would be possible to catch a bus back to Birmingham,
complete with bikes. This idea certainly appealed to them as it
meant less mileage.

They were shown to a telephone, just outside the kitchen, and
here they phoned the bus company to find if their newly found
information was correct. Unfortunately they had great difficulty
in hearing anything at all, owing to two Italian chefs having an
argument over the bus timetable. However, after fifteen minutes
of unnecessary conversation, it at last transpired that the bus
would not take bikes, and so the whole operation was a waste of
time. They were both rather annoyed at the considerable delay,
which had evolved around the telephone call, especially as they
had a train to catch, and so they bade the chefs (still arguing)
goodbye, and hurried off.

About two miles further on they descended down a steep hill
which led all the way to Hereford, and were able to free wheel
for three and a half miles. This pleased them both immensely
as they had both decided that they needed a well-earned rest.

On arrival mummy decided that she did not like the heavy
traffic thundering past her, and so got off her bike and walked.

Anne, not wanting to miss anything, also dismounted and they both ended up walking the last mile to the station. Owing to all the delays *en route* they missed the train by ten minutes, which involved a long wait of an hour and a half before the next train to Birmingham. They spent this time arguing with a porter about the fate of their bicycles. He decided that no labels were needed to tie on them, but they decided the opposite. Eventually they won, and he grudgingly threw two labels at them. After they had proudly tied these on their handlebars, as a sign of victory, they entered the canteen to repair their hurt pride.

After a long wait the train eventually drew in. They both went frantic because there were no porters in sight to transfer the bikes from platform to train. Feeling desperate they both picked up mummy's bike and carried it along the platform whilst trying to find the guard's van. As they could not locate it they had to carry the bike all the way back again. To their horror, Anne's bike had disappeared. Suddenly a cheery voice hailed them and looking around they saw a red face peering at them from the guard's van. They then caught sight of Anne's bike buried under four sacks of mail. Picking up mummy's bike once more they ran to the van and hoisted it in. They gave their instructions to the guard concerning their dear bikes, and then leapt into the train.

At Worcester station a crowd of schoolgirls entered the train and seated themselves with a lot of noise. As A and M viewed them with interest, they heard one girl remark, 'Are they boys?' This sent them both into convulsions and they felt most indignant.

The tickets showed them that they should leave the train at Stourbridge station, but on stopping at Hagley they decided that it would be more convenient if they got off there, and so jumped out quickly. The guard's van was approached and the guard was asked for the bikes. He went completely berserk! He yelled and shouted and they finally understood that he disapproved of the arrangement. He told them that they were unable to remove their bikes, as they had not reached their destination. Not wanting to waste time they jumped quickly into the van, threw the mail sacks on the floor and grabbed their bikes. The guard was completely taken aback and stood watching helplessly as they pedalled into the darkness.

Soon they joined the M5 service road leading past Clent. It was not lit and the lamps of the cars cast terrifying patterns on the tarmac road. After about a quarter of a mile mummy stopped and shrieked at Anne saying that she could not cycle any longer. It transpired that she couldn't see and kept pedalling onto the pavement. After this explanation, they walked. Rednal was six miles away and Anne at least had no intention of walking that far at 9 p.m. and so decided to leave her bike at the garage, which was two miles further on. Those two miles were spent persuading mummy to do the same. Eventually mummy agreed.

The garage was quickly reached and their bikes abandoned. They both felt absolute traitors to the YHA but were determined not to pedal an inch further. They located a telephone and rang daddy asking him to come and collect them in the car. He came and they were taken back to Rednal in style. Precisely one week later, their bikes were fetched and their holiday was completed.

St Briavels

Two hostellers stood at the castle gate,
The night was dark and the hour was late.
Into the prison they were shown,
Just the two of them alone.
Time passed by and they moved out,
Thought there were some ghosts about.
Moved their bedding, sheets and all,
Crept into the corridor.
Into the hangman's room they scurried,
Looked at the gibbet and to bed they hurried.
Their teeth chattered and they began quaking,
Before very long they both were shaking.
The gibbet attracted them and they kept spying,
At the chasm in the wall near where they were lying.
Anne turned over and went to sleep,
M just lay there afraid to peep.
Midnight came and so did tapping,
Sounded like somebody rapping.
Anne awoke and looked around,
But she never heard a sound.
Dawn eventually broke.
In the light it seemed a joke.
Until later on they met three more,
Who'd also heard knocking on the prison door.
These were in fact no idle boasts,
But some real live ghosts.
They returned home the very next morn,
All their friends they then did warn.

Margaret and Clive formed a very successful rambling club in
the 1980s which operated from Our Lady of Perpetual Succour
in Rednal. It was there that they met Frances and decided to go
'one step further'.

From North to South along Offa's Dyke
Lower Spoad Farm, Clun to Hay-on-Wye
Approximately 45 miles

From Saturday 14 May to Thursday 19 May 1983

After discussing the possibility of walking Offa's Dyke in the dim
distant future, F, C and M on Thursday, 11 May 1983 suddenly
sprang into action and started preparations in earnest for the
venture. Their first call was the YHA shop where they joined.
(Once again M regretted not becoming a life member in 1934
at the price of £5.00.) It was now £50.00 for life membership.
The yearly fee was £5.00 plus £1.95 for seniors (which they all
were) for a simple hostel, and up to £2.75 for a standard hostel.
Never mind, M felt that it was good to be back in the YHA
movement once again, forty-nine years later, feeling quite as
young at heart as ever, but not quite so young physically! They
purchased sundry articles such as money belts, further maps –
they had hundreds already – and a slab each of Kendal mint
cake to help them survive *en route* in case of any calamity, plus
water bottles to slake their thirst. On arrival home M booked
three beds for the night of 14 May at Knighton Youth Hostel.
Haversacks were packed and unpacked many times; articles,
which at one stage were thought to be absolutely essential were
later abandoned, but even so their packs seemed to weigh tons,

but there it was – very difficult when it was necessary to carry all one's requirements on one's back.

The forecast was pretty gloomy – following about five weeks of rain; in fact the wettest April on record, and May following the same pattern. They were all to make a very early start as they were catching the eight o'clock coach from Birmingham to join the E.J.S. Ramblers, and walking from Lower Spoad Farm near Clun, to Knighton. Consequently none of them had a very good night as they were all frightened of oversleeping and missing the bus. Anyway all's well that ends well, and they all gathered at the meeting place on time, somewhat bleary eyed, still pondering on whether they were wearing the right clothes, but then too late to do anything about it.

Fifty-three of them boarded the coach, many of them carrying packs quite as large as F C and M's, just for one day's walking which worried F, C and M somewhat as their luggage was for a whole week! They stopped for coffee at Hundred House, Purslow, and consumed lots of biscuits as there were plates of them on every table. By this time it was raining – quite torrential – and their spirits sank, but by the time they reached Lower Spoad Farm the sun was shining, and they set off in high spirits southwards along the Dyke, up Spoad Hill to Llanfair Hill with magnificent views all around. The walking was pretty steep at times – quite a lot of it actually along the dyke itself. The wind was very rough, but they did get quite a lot of sunshine. They had to take their own lunches as civilization was a long way off their luncheon stop, and by this time it was raining quite heavily, but fortunately there was a barn handy, and they all trooped thankfully into this.

The members, ranged in five tiers on the bales, were quite a sight to behold. By the time they had finished lunch, the rain had almost stopped, and they sallied forth bedecked in their cagoules, hats and gloves, as a very strong wind was blowing.

The route was very muddy over Cwm-sanaham Hill and Panpauton Hill. They descended into Knighton down an extremely steep slope, causing their toes to be crammed into their boots and much havoc and pain to their knees. Having reached the bottom of the hill they walked by the bank of the River Teme only to be confronted by another steep climb up lots of steps to the town. M by this time, at the end of her tether frantically hunted for a toilet; F vanished inside the information centre and C disappeared altogether!

After much searching, they all ended up at the Coffee Shop and had a really sumptuous tea of sandwiches, scones, cakes and lots of cuppas (coffee for F as always). The Coffee House was presided over by Mrs Barbara Webb and Mrs June Noble, who was the widow of Frank Noble, the well-known pioneer of the Offa's Dyke route; two most charming ladies with equally charming daughters. C ended up at a different table from F and M, but his booming voice resounded throughout the building, so they knew that he was under the same roof, which was important to M as he had the money for the tea! Maybe the charming daughters had something to do with his absence – who knows? After tea they bade farewell to their fellow ramblers who, with one accord, wished them well and booked in at the hostel. C and M felt quite at home and F, although never having done it before, quickly settled in. F, on removing her boots, discovered that she had walked eight miles that day with two aspirins in her boot! No wonder she was suffering somewhat as their pain-killing propensities do not work unless taken internally. 'Nuf said.

The girls' (please note *girls*) dormitory was quite nice. Only five of them in it. M instructed F on how to make up the beds; they chose top bunks right opposite the toilet (for easy access during the night), washed their muddy boots in the wash-basins – strictly against the rules but what else could they do? and then sallied forth to find the Catholic church. After enquiring of sundry residents who hadn't the slightest idea where the church was, they decided to consult the police, but *en route* to the police station they met Nancy who escorted them to the church right at the top of a very steep hill. Knighton was built on a hill so wherever one went it was either up or down – never on the level. By the time they reached the church they were all consumed with thirst, so called in at The Plough and had two drinks apiece and heard the life history of the proprietress – all very interesting – making a date for lunch the next day after Mass.

They returned to the hostel to try and phone for accommodation the following night. The one address was fully booked, and no reply from two others, so in a state of mild panic they managed to book two rooms at Pilleth Court, near Whitton, despite the fact that it was about two miles off the path which would add four miles to their journey the following day. Still, it was a relief to get booked in and so avoid the possibility of having to tramp the Dyke through the night. They all retired to bed at about 10.30 p.m. but F and M had great difficulty in mounting the top bunks. M had definitely lost the 'spring' required to reach up top. However, with the help of a chair, and much puffing and blowing they ascended, were very warm and comfortable, both of them lying underneath six blankets apiece, and not even having to descend to get to the loo.

Torrential rain greeted them on waking up, but after a good breakfast of cereal, bacon and tomato, bread and butter and marmalade, their spirits rose as the sun came out, and they wandered into the town to buy postcards to send home and to attend 11.30 Mass. They purchased the cards, and the sun was so warm by this time, that they sat in the picnic area by the river writing them, and then walked up the hill to the church. On arrival they discovered that Mass was at 11.45. The priest had three parishes to serve and they altered the time of Mass to give him a little more time. It was a lovely little church and M met a lady from Alvechurch who had retired there with her friend eleven years ago. They said what a lively and friendly place Knighton was, in need of more Catholics and they wished that they would retire there too!

After Mass they met Ian, Anne and the boys, went into The Plough for lunch, and afterwards set off on the Dyke Path towards their overnight stay at Pilleth Court. By this time it was raining again and the climb out of Knighton was very steep, but the dyke was clearly marked all the way. Ian took some photographs of them all which should prove to look quite hilarious they thought!

The weather was pretty showery all day but they had sunshine too, and the views and skyscapes were truly glorious. Martin walked along so quickly that he disappeared into the distance and was eventually located three fields ahead – a little speck in the distance. However he was recalled and Ian and family returned to their car waiting for them in Knighton. F, M and

On the Dyke above Knighton

C plodded on quite happily, but as mentioned before, had to leave the path to get to their accommodation. They could see the village of Whitton just below them but had to take a circuitous route of about three miles to get there along hard road, and quite frankly they were all at the end of their tethers on arrival, having walked that afternoon about seven miles. But it proved to be a super place, full of the most lovely antiques, and Mrs Hood provided them with egg on toast (beans for C) and lovely fresh cream gateau with oodles of tea to drink. Afterwards they talked with the family, watched part of *That's Life* and eventually sank

Viewing the scene –the Dyke

into bed aching in every limb and feeling that the only solution was to hightail it for home first thing the next day. *However*, after a wonderful night's rest and a lovely breakfast with the sun shining, their spirits soared and once again they felt able to face the rigours of the day. The bill was most reasonable, bed and breakfast, supper and sandwiches – £8.25 each.

On Monday morning, 16th May, they bade farewell to Mrs Hood and luck was on their side as Mr Hood was going their way and gave them a lift in his farm vehicle (F and M had great difficulty in climbing up front while C bumped along quite

happily in the back amongst the straw, etc.) to the path just past
Dolley Green, which saved them the extra three miles they had
walked the previous evening. The route was well sign-posted but
they hadn't been long on the way when they had to go through a
field housing a fierce-looking huge white bull. As there were calves
in the field too, F and M were absolutely terrified, as neither of
them was capable of running, owing to their tired and stiff limbs,
plus the muddy conditions, so had the bull charged them they
were resigned to being tossed and pawed or whatever irate bulls
do to humans. M marched resolutely through the field looking,
neither to right nor left while F kept casting glances at the beast
saying in frantic tones 'He's staring at us'. Eventually however,
they made for the gate opposite without mishap having had to
negotiate thick gooey mud in order to get through.

They had lunch in a very sheltered spot near a quarry, each
of them sitting on quite a substantial flat stone. On rising F
discovered she had broken hers; she must have put on weight to
break such a solid seat. As they finished their lunch it started
to rain and thunder was resounding around the hills in a most
ominous manner. The view was fantastic over to Herrick Hill.

On approaching Burfa House M was overcome by thirst – as
was her wont – and pleaded with C that he should request some
cold water. He bravely marched up to the front door which
was opened by an old lady who didn't seem to be quite 'with it'.
However, C handed over his water bottle which was eventually
returned, filled with water but minus the stopper. This was
requested and back she went into her kitchen to find it, returning
once again to say it was nowhere to be seen! She did however invite
M in to have a look. The kitchen was a sight to behold – dirty

dishes and clutter everywhere – plus one very elderly husband who was blandly sitting among the chaos happily drinking a cup of tea. After much searching M found the stopper lying at the bottom of the sink. On leaving they read signs indicating that pots of tea, lemonade, bed & breakfast, Camping on the lawn, etc., were available, and they all assumed this information appertained to the house next door – Hen Burfa, a restored medieval house. By this time it was really pouring down and thundering as well, so they decided to have a cuppa and take shelter. The door was opened by a very superior lady who said that she herself did not do refreshments but that the lady next door did – the house they had just left. Having seen the state of the kitchen they did not fancy anything to eat or drink there, so began to wend their way onwards. Overcome by remorse and guilt at their sorry state, the superior lady called them back and provided them with a lovely pot of tea, and coffee for F for which they only paid 50p. On rising up to leave M suddenly missed her Navy Blue Holdall containing purse, glasses, these notes, etc., and remembered that she had left it on the bench outside Burfa House when she had gone in to look for the missing stopper. Fortunately it was still where she had left it, although the bag and contents were absolutely sodden.

The weather improved somewhat *en route* and they started to climb up the side of the hill to the ridge of the Dyke between Rushock and Herrock hills. Usually, on reaching the top of a steep ascent, they noticed an even steeper hill on the other side of the valley which invariably had to be climbed, but this time they dropped steeply into Kington via the golf course, with the prospect of the steep hill opposite to be coped with the next morning. They had been given an address at Kington by a Mr Daly – a walker – where he had stayed the previous night, but prior to reaching Kington, they stopped to converse with a charming young man from Gloucester, who was walking alone up to Ruthin, and when in sight of the actual town F 'brewed up' and they thoroughly enjoyed a warm drink.

Kington looked only a short distance away but, as always, at the end of the day every step seemed like a mile. However on reaching Glen Arrow, Victoria Road, nothing could have exceeded the kind welcome given to them by Mrs Mills. Their wet and muddy boots were removed and later cleaned by Andrew and they were presented with tea and cake. Lovely bedrooms with hot and cold, and even a toilet for the sole use of C and M. They sank to rest, having walked eight miles in, as yet, completely unspoilt country, nearly all of it well farmed. Here again they thought the terms reasonable – £7.00 each including B&B and packed lunches.

They were greeted the next morning with the patter of rain drops and the glorious smell of bacon, etc., but by the time they had finished breakfast the sun was shining and they sallied forth once again in high spirits. Sundry purchases were made in the town, and C, full of confidence, led them out of Kington on the way, as he told them, to Newchurch, their next overnight stopping place. M, all the time felt uneasy, being certain that they were on the wrong route, but with her usual inferiority complex and diffident manner, having been schooled to think C was never wrong, kept silent. After only a short while fortunately C discovered his error so they retraced their steps to the Square to start again. Standing in the Square was a bus going to Hereford.

M was slightly tempted – had it been still raining no doubt she would have succumbed – but F and C obviously never gave defeat a second thought so M bravely thrust temptation away and battled on.

The path took them over Hergest Ridge – the views were wonderful there and the contrasts of light and shade beautiful; the sound of singing larks and other birds and the sheep were slightly marred by the zooming of Phantom Jets overhead, which were really very frightening and noisy, but even this they got used to, as it was an area where much practice took place in low flying.

They descended to Gladestry where they had a most welcome rest and drink at the Royal Oak. M took the opportunity of removing her tights in exchange for socks and attended to her toes. Once again they had to climb steeply out of the village but the sun was shining and they enjoyed Mrs Mills' sandwiches for lunch. As soon as they had finished, it began to rain and for the rest of the day they plodded on through waterlogged fields all the way to Baynham House. Just before reaching it they passed a farm barn outside which was a tap – this was about the only time M was not thirsty – over which was a very funny picture of a very fat lady walker, and the following poem which the farmer copied out for them as they did not have a camera:

> If you are walking Offa's Dyke,
> And this should catch your eye;
> If your pack is feeling heavy,
> And your throat is feeling dry.
> There's water flowing in this tap,
> It's cool, it's fresh, it's free;

It may not be as strong as wine,
But neither is the fee!
You may imbibe the elixir,
Avoiding spill or waste,
And having thus refreshed yourself,
Be on your way with haste.

The farmer then advised them to take the short cut to Baynham House thus avoiding a very steep hill, but, as the route was on the lower slopes, the mud was dreadful through which they wallowed for at least three quarters of a mile, and they literally fell into the entrance hall at about 5.30 p.m. with everything soaking wet, even the contents of their haversacks.

They felt that they were a little earlier than expected, but eventually they were given a nice cuppa and shown to their rooms – nice but somewhat chilly. After they had changed into dry things Mrs Croose lit a lovely log fire in the lounge and they sat down to a scrumptious dinner of home-cured ham, mashed potatoes, peas, salad, rhubarb tart and custard and coffee. It was absolutely lovely – but still the rain poured down! Whatever would it be like in the morning they wondered! Mrs Croose has six children and C played chess with the youngest child, a lovely little girl called Jane, aged about ten. F had her brewing session of hot chocolate in the bedroom, and, despite the chilliness, they all had a comfortable night's rest. They again had a lovely breakfast (cost of everything was £10.25) and thus fortified they set out for Hay-on-Wye, not being quite certain as to whether to return from Hay or face the rigours of the Black Mountains, the problem being scanty accommodation *en route*. Only time would tell! But they did feel, at that moment, that after yesterday's rain the going would be worse than ever. Even their boots were not standing up to the waterlogged fields. The country had had the wettest April on record and so far the wettest May!

At this juncture F complained of sore shoulders owing to the rubbing of her haversack straps, but she was padded underneath with M's vest and pants, and on top with foam strips given to her by Mrs Croose, and feeling much more comfortable, they once again set off – unbelievably in sunshine.

They walked into Newchurch by road on account of the muddy conditions on the hills, and then over Little Mountain, and eventually dropped down to Bettws Dingle and on through woods, tracks and many fields – all muddy. Eventually after many stiles they arrived on the banks of the Wye and Clyro Bridge which took them into Hay.

As the weather had been warm and sunny they were all consumed with thirst, but their first quest was to find accommodation. The first address they knew had a sign in the window 'No Vacancies', so in a slight panic they rushed to the next bed and breakfast sign and booked in. Mrs P. Cochrane, Clifton House, Belmont Road. Mrs Cochrane was out, but the daughter asked them to sign the register and then informed them that F would have to pay the full fee of £12.00 as she was having a twin-bedded room; unless she wished to recline on one of the bunk beds in C and M's room. Naturally she didn't want to do this and so resigned herself to paying this extortionate fee. M decided that Mrs Cochrane was a commercial shark on the make, and was seething with indignation at this injustice, determined to confront Mrs C on this point in the morning.

They went out for drinks where they met two Welshmen from Sennybridge who were out on a coach outing. They were both widowers and one had a daughter at Selly Oak Hospital who lectured on biology and was married to a brain surgeon. They could only understand what one of them was saying; the other was somewhat inarticulate, but they all said 'Yes' and 'No' in what they hoped were the right places and tried to look intelligent. They then decided to buy some fish and chips and to eat them out of the paper in truly glorious fashion, but by this time it was raining again, so they entered the restaurant and ate them in elite fashion off a plate. After that they returned to Clifton House and so to bed. The clock outside the house struck every quarter of an hour; C slept the sleep of the just; so too F after her brewing-up session, but M was kept awake, partly by the chiming of the clock, and partly by the preparation of her speech to Mrs Cochrane the next morning. Anyway she consumed a Mars bar at 2.15 a.m. and thereafter slept well.

The next morning M confronted Mrs Cochrane and asked her if it was correct that F had had to pay double; M pointed out that they had not had any further enquiries for a room that night – that was a shot in the dark but M was pretty sure they hadn't. Mrs C said that she had been thinking about the matter and would only charge F the usual £6.00 so she was restored to favour in M's eyes, and in view of that, they might even stay there again when they returned to Hay later in the year – when they hoped – to recommence their walking Offa's Dyke.

By the time breakfast was over, it was pouring with rain; no sign of the mountains whatsoever as the clouds were so low, and in view of the accommodation problem they decided to return home. They caught the 9.45 bus to Hereford; stopped to have a cuppa and a scone, and then caught the 12.25 train to New Street. A slight improvement in the weather but still dull.

This had been a momentous few days for F, C and M – something of everything, and there was no doubt that they would *never* be *quite* the same again. The pleasure was derived, not only from seeing such beautiful scenery and experiencing peace and relaxation, but from the chance meetings with all sorts of types of humanity – bed and breakfast ladies and their families, hostellers, fellow ramblers, farmers, etc. It was hoped to be able to continue these memoirs on the next step of their journey along Offa's Dyke.

After this strenuous trek C and M found they were heavier by half a stone in weight. Fate can be cruel!

Details of approx. expenditure for holiday walking Offa's Dyke from Lower Spoad Farm to Hay-on-Wye from 14th–19th May 1983 for two

	Expenditure		Sub-total
14 May: 9 miles Lower Spoad Farm to Kington	Coach fare Drinks Tea at Knighton Youth hostel Telephone calls	£5.40 £1.40 £2.40 £4.80 £0.30	£14.30
15 May: 7½ miles Knighton to Pilleth Court, Whitton	Lunch at Knighton Drinks Supper, B&B, packed lunch	£2.40 £0.70 £16.50	£19.60
16 May: 8 miles Pilleth Court to Kington	Tea at Burfa House Telephone calls Drinks at Royal Oak, Gladestry Supper, B&B, packed lunch (Mrs Mills)	£0.50 £0.10 £1.40 £14.00	£16.00
17 May: 9 miles Kington to Baynham Hall Farm	Dinner, B&B, packed lunch	£20.50	£20.50
18 May: 9 miles Baynham Hall Farm to Hay-on-Wye	Meal in Hay–on-Wye Drinks B&B Hay-on-Wye	£3.36 £0.58 £12.00	£15.94
19 May: return home Hay-on-Wye to Birmingham	Bus to Hereford Refreshments Left luggage Train to Birmingham	£3.30 £1.13 £0.50 £7.00	£11.93
		Total	**£98.27**

Total mileage: 42½ miles

Second Installment of the Walk along Offa's Dyke
Hay-on-Wye to Brockweir, Approximately Fifty Miles

3–9 October 1983

As October approached – the month earmarked for F, C and M to finish walking the southern part of Offa's Dyke, C and M, in view of very heavy expense on the car – decided that they could not afford to do the whole trip right down to Chepstow. However, as time passed by, and the date of their departure approached, they decided to even risk bankruptcy to finish the southern half of the walk and so M, with utter abandon, withdrew all her year's interest without a backward look. The date of departure was still undecided – they were waiting for the new moon, long range weather forecast, and anything else they thought might help, before they definitely decided on a date, but they did intend driving to Hereford, leaving the car in Ian's bus garage and Anne would drive them on to Hay-on-Wye – their starting point.

On 20 September they all embarked on a B.M.I. (Birmingham Midland Institute) trip around Birmingham on an open-topped bus, with lunch to follow, when they intended discussing final details of the trip. After the bus ride they arrived back at the B.M.I., absolutely frozen to the marrow, looking forward to a nice hot lunch, only to be confronted by a cold buffet – not even a hot drink. They decided to concentrate on finalising plans over a hot coffee in the restaurant proper. For reasons unknown, they were overcome by mirth and hilarious laughter, but then got down to seriously planning their holiday being unable to decide whether to start on Saturday 1 October, or Monday, the 3rd. After much deliberation the Monday was decided upon but F was so bemused by it all, that on making her exit from the B.M.I. she did not seem to know where she was or even where she was going. However they all parted company on New Street precinct, arranging for F to arrive at 165 Leach Green Lane on Monday at twelve o'clock. M then phoned Anne to arrange for transport to Hay whereupon their plans had once more to be altered to fit in with Anne's commitments. A further call to F arranging once and for all for her to be at 165 at 10 o'clock on the Monday morning, equipped with packed lunch which they proposed eating in Hay-on-Wye – weather permitting, of course!

The weather previous to their holiday was dreadful. Nothing but rain, mist and fog. Their spirits were at a very low level and in desperation M phoned F, who had telephoned Cardiff for the long range weather forecast which pointed to some improvement on Monday, but the uncertainty of the outlook made them feel very undecided as to whether to go or not. They all decided to listen to the Farming forecast on Sunday to see if that would help. It didn't; it was pretty awful.

On Monday 3 October, the scheduled day of their departure, the heavens just opened and rain poured down. C and M were expecting a phone call any minute from F postponing the trip. F was likewise expecting one from C and M. The phone rang.

'This is it,' said M to C. They both decided to abide by what they were sure would be F's decision to postpone things, only to discover that it was Elva on the end of the line. Preparations for packing and cutting sandwiches went on apace when the phone rang again. 'Oh no!' said C in horrified tones. But this time it was Frances who seemed really amazed that they were even contemplating departure. F arrived, looking somewhat wet and bedraggled, and they eventually set off, after fortifying themselves with coffee to revive their drooping spirits.

By 10.45 a.m. happily the rain had stopped and they began to feel a little brighter. M's first port of call was the building society to obtain the wherewithal; after which they careered off down the M5 to Hereford. Tramp gave them a noisy greeting, and after securing their money around their persons, with Anne at the wheel, they set off to Hay-on-Wye. They bade Anne a fond farewell at the car park, and there they were – all three of them – abandoned and forlorn with nothing in the world with them but their very weighty haversacks.

All rather bemused they wandered along to the children's playground, where M remembered from her distant past, were benches, where they could sit to eat their lunch. On arriving, not a bench was in sight, so they spread themselves on a bench on the main road to eat their lunch and drink their cuppas, hoping no one would pass who would recognise them. Believe it or not the sun came out and it was really warm and pleasant. However this was not to last for long and before they had finished a slight drizzle set in, so they made their way to Belmont House where they were booked in for the night. This proved to be a warm, comfortable and friendly place; they endeavoured to get organised and later set off to tour the town happily without their heavy haversacks.

Hay was quite a confusing place and they wandered hither and thither, up and down lots of steps, in and out of shops buying postcards and sustenance for the morrow, and decided eventually to have their evening meal at the Black Lion, a thirteenth-century inn. As usual M was consumed with thirst, which even an ice cream did not slake. By 4 p.m. they sank to rest on a bench outside the 'Largest Bookshop in the World', to await opening time at the Black Lion at 6.00 p.m. The thought of lemon and lime filled M's mind and she just longed for 6 p.m.

At about 4.30 M could stand her thirst no longer so they all took refuge in The Granary, imbibing tea and coffee until nearly 6 p.m. As it was by this time drizzling outside this really was a haven of refuge. From The Granary they repaired to The Black Lion, and ordered the much longed for lime and lemon – lager for C – until 7.00 p.m. when meals were served. They were rather astonished at the prices, but throwing caution to the winds ordered salad for C and M and chicken and chips for F – all very nice. About 8.00 p.m. they wended their way back to Belmont House where they were given the lounge at their disposal plus television and gas fire. By this time the weather was rather damp but not actually raining.

Next morning (Tuesday, 4 Oct.) their eyes opened to quite a pleasant morning, somewhat cloudy but fairly bright. C and M slept in the most extraordinary coloured sheets, white with green butterflies and trailing creepers all over them; they felt they were sleeping in a greenhouse but nevertheless all three had a very good night, ready to meet whatever might befall them that day. After a very good breakfast of grapefruit, bacon, egg, sausage, mushrooms and fried bread, plus toast and marmalade, they set off at 9.30 in glorious sunshine. M decided at this point that all her wardrobe was wrong – too hot! At least they were booked in at Capel-y-ffin Youth Hostel for the night, so they had no worries on that score, although after that they had no idea at all where they would be resting their weary forms. Only time would tell!

After shopping in Hay for bread, milk, bacon and apples they set off. They decided to take the road as it was their first day and they did think the fields might be muddy. Also the thought of *bulls* was very much to the forefront of F and M's minds. It was a long pretty hard climb up from Hay, but the views were glorious and the weather too. They stopped for coffee and biscuits at 11.20 on a pleasant grassy bank by the roadside, just past New Forest Farm, sheltered from the wind which by this time was blowing quite strong.

On leaving this delightful spot they still climbed upwards and passed around the base of Hay Bluff. As they ascended, the silence was shattered by loud thuds and bangs and they came across two rather rough-looking men overturning a car down the bank. As they climbed upwards a hippy commune came into view; there were about fifty old cars, buses and caravans littered all over the place absolutely desecrating one of the most beautiful parts of the Offa's Dyke path. Apparently they moved in about a fortnight before and the council were trying to get them moved but apparently this was easier said than done. Clive was invited in to have a cup of tea but politely refused. They did seem to be running a snack bar of sorts but goodness knows where they obtained fresh, clean water! They doubted if many people would stop there as the whole set-up looked dirty and grotty.

As they approached the top of the Gospel Pass they faced a terrific head wind – gale force – and for at least two miles they battled against this whilst climbing all the time. C kept encouraging F and M by saying it would be better when they got round the corner, but was it? Not on your life! M kept her

Brewing up

eyes focussed on the ground so that she could not see the climb in front of her, but eventually they did reach the top and as they began to descend the wind did abate somewhat, although it was still fairly strong. They were able to find a fairly sheltered spot for lunch, which consisted of bread and butter, cheese, apple and Mars bar plus the proverbial cup of tea (coffee for F.)

By the time they had finished this repast it was only 2.30 p.m. and they only had about two miles to go to the youth hostel. (Throughout the trip it was discovered that they covered the miles far quicker than they thought they would.)

They proceeded further down the Vale of Ewys and M wrote these notes overlooking the Black Mountains in lovely sunshine, the silence only broken by the wind in the trees, the croaking of a bird of prey, and the bleating of the sheep. This was a very remote and most beautiful valley, and was particularly peaceful and relaxing. As they were resting a rather peculiar rambler spoke to them; he had the normal haversack, but was resplendent in mauve ear-rings; not the usual garb for walkers. He said he was worn out having walked sixteen miles from Raglan and that he was going on to Hay, another seven. F and M had the feeling that he had hitch-hiked most of the way, but maybe they did him an injustice. He was nick-named Flash Harry. When he informed C that he also had with him a bottle of brandy and one of whisky, they all decided that he was on his way to join the hippie commune, where they were sure he would be most welcome!

After this interlude they proceeded downhill and arrived at the hostel very early, but had to wait until 5.00 p.m. to enter. The wind had turned rather cold and strong by this time, and they were glad to get inside at the appropriate time. Just before going inside their glances moved upwards to the top of the pass, where outlined against the sky was what appeared to be a huge crowd of people! Liking hostels to themselves they hoped the crowd was not making its way to Capel-y-ffin, but on booking in they were informed that a school party had been in residence for the past three days and were at that moment coming down the hill. They felt shattered, but of course hostellers cannot be selfish and have to take the rough with the smooth. The going this time was rough! F and M selected bunks on the landing while C was closeted in an attic with at least fourteen schoolboys. Poor C! F and M were at least the only two occupants of the landing, so they selected top bunks and spread all their luggage on the bottom bunks. This all had to be gathered up on the arrival of two girls from Australia, but they turned out to be very nice and quite interesting.

On the arrival of the kids all hell seemed to be let loose. They were so incredibly noisy, but on the whole they were well behaved. F, C and M had ordered cooked supper and this was eaten with the children in the common room. It was quite appetizing, consisting of vegetable soup, chicken supreme with rice, tomatoes and peas, followed by apple crumble and custard and tea or coffee. Once the meal was over the noise became louder than ever. F's nerves were badly shattered and so they decided to get ready for bed about 9.30 and got washed and undressed in some privacy, before the avalanche of kids took possession of the only three wash-basins and two toilets provided for the female population. Facilities at this hostel were most inadequate and on the whole was decidedly 'crumby'

The children eventually retired to bed and all was quiet at about 10.30, but not for long. Some of them cried out in their sleep, others coughed, and there seemed to be a constant procession of children down the dark stairs to the toilets below. It was a wonder nobody fell down them as the stairs were very steep and unlit. Through it all M – had quite a good night, but

F's shattered nervous system would not allow her to sleep, and she rose at about 7.00 a.m. rather the worse for wear.

They cooked their own breakfast – cornflakes, bacon and egg (which M overcooked) and bread. They did their jobs of cleaning the Members' kitchen, their dormitory, and sweeping the yard, and were ready to leave at 9.50 a.m. amid absolute chaos as all the children were leaving that day and didn't seem able to find any of their belongings. However F, C and M left them all to it, and thankfully beat a hasty retreat, breathing in the fresh mountain air to rid them of the rather acrid smell of the hostel. It was a great pity that this hostel was such a *dump*, as it was very remote and set in some of the most beautiful scenery imaginable.

Wednesday (5th), the weather was lovely – just perfect for walking, being cloudy with sunny intervals and a gentle breeze blowing. Their journey took them still down the Vale of Ewys and they walked steadily reaching Llanthony at 11.30 a.m. There was something in the air of that place which seemed to have a profound effect on one; the spiritual atmosphere one would imagine!

They made their way to the Abbey Hotel and started off with lime and lemon, lager for C followed by coffee for F and tea for C and M. For some unknown reason F was served with a biscuit; not so C and M so C dived into his haversack and C and M blatantly ate their own. Also having coffee was a gentleman accompanied by two rather elderly and precise-looking dames; he seemed to be looking at F, C and M with interest and obvious envy. When they rose to leave his curiosity overcame him, and advancing towards them enquired where they had come from and to where were they going. He said that he had joined the

YHA two years before but couldn't embark on anything quite so strenuous as walking Offa's Dyke. F and M decided that C was most fortunate with *his* dames, and they all felt distinctly noble and swelled with pride at their achievements! Two photographs were taken and they set out once more for the Lancaster Arms at Pandy.

After some distance they left the road to take a field path. M knocked on a cottage door to enquire about *bulls*, but was told that all was well. On reaching a suitable lunch spot they started to enjoy their repast of bread and butter, cheese, chocolate, apples and tea, when a horse, browsing in the field, sauntered across to them and tried to eat everything in sight, including their anoraks and haversacks. F gave up trying to get a drink so they packed everything up and left the poor old horse alone in his field looking sorrowfully after them. On approaching the next field they found it full of cows, but was there a bull among them – that was the question? M espied a farmer coming towards them – heaven sent – who thought they had lost their way. M enquired if there was a bull in the field.

'Oh yes,' said the farmer, 'that white fellow over there!'

Their eyes alighted on a huge beast who certainly did look mild enough, but remembering the old adage 'Never trust a bull' M asked the farmer if he would accompany them across. He willingly did so but actually was going their way in any case. The bull did not even raise its ugly head, but what would have been their unhappy fate had he seen them and they had not been accompanied? Who knows!

On they went through beautiful fields and managed to pass their turning. C realised his error so back they went and shortly saw the familiar Offa's Dyke signpost. That never failed to thrill them as they knew that they were on the right path. A stop was made on top of a grassy bank for drinks, and then down to the Lancaster Arms at Pandy, over two fields and the railway line.

They received a nice welcome; repaired to their rooms in a somewhat exhausted state, by this time aching all over. It occurred to M that she may be utilising the bus stop to Hereford the next morning, which was right opposite the Lancaster Arms. They had dinner about 8.00 p.m. Ham, chips, salad, apple tart for C; strawberry flan for F and M – all very nice. M then had a hot bath hoping for relief from her aches and pains. Only the morning would tell. They all had a view of Skirrid from their bedroom windows which was lovely, but as a ladies darts match was being organised for that night, they were warned that there would be plenty of noise until at least midnight. Whatever noise there was, however, they slept soundly through it, and after a breakfast of bacon, egg and tomato, they set off equipped with packed lunch (at the exorbitant price of £1.25 each for two rolls and an apple). They set off on the path to Llantilio Crossenny where they had arranged to be met at the Hostry Inn and taken on to Llandewi Rhydderch, where they had booked in for evening meal, bed and breakfast at Keeper's Cottage run by Julie and Andrew Paxton. They did feel on leaving the Lancaster Arms, that Doreen Taylor (the proprietress) could not get rid of them quickly enough – however they had been very comfortable while staying with her.

Thursday (6th). Their journey took them through many fields and over lots and lots of stiles (these were a feature of the path,) and on arrival at St Cadoc's Church they decided to have their elevenses in the porch. As usual they all signed the visitors' book in the church and then continued on their way. Their journey was quite uneventful until the path led them through a field housing cows, calves and at least *two mightly bulls* who glared at them with fierce looks as they leaned over the gate contemplating what on earth to do! The farm nearby seemed empty and derelict,

All packed and ready to go

although two dogs kept barking round their heels, but there was no sign of any friendly farmer to escort them through. They were all adamant that no way were they going through that field and miraculously they made a detour around an adjoining field and eventually came out on the right path and the familiar Offa's Dyke signpost. That was really due to C's superb brilliant leadership and sense of direction. M doesn't possess this; F does.

They had their lunch by a stream in a field without any cattle for a change; weather was nice – and then onward past White Castle which was in a wonderful state of preservation. An extremely muddy path had to be negotiated. After leaving White Castle poor F collapsed in a heap, at the same time grasping a handful of stinging nettles! She felt the pain from this accident for hours. She recovered from this mishap only later on to fall over a tussock in a field – they were all trying to hurry through a herd of cows – right into a cow pat! She was obviously somewhat accident prone and as events so often went in threes C and M were wondering what the next mishap will be. Not F's lucky day!

They perched themselves on a convenient tree-trunk for a cuppa and the cows from the field they had just left meandered over to them in curiosity. Onward to The Hostelry at Llantilio Crossenny to phone the Paxtons. A very cultured voice answered M who weighed them up to be very modern and arty crafty. She was quite correct in this assumption. Andrew met them accompanied by one of the children – Lucy aged four – a somewhat precocious child who called her father, Andrew. They did wonder whether he was her father as there did seem to be something a little odd about the relationship. C, F and M felt there was some mystery somewhere but never found out what it was; perhaps it existed just in their imaginations. The other two boys were Ben, aged ten, and a baby, aged two.

Keeper's Cottage was over a hundred years old and was being restored to order by Andrew. The staircase was in process of being ripped out and much banging and knocking was the result. Julie was obviously very arty and the whole place was full of old pictures, dried flowers, shawls draping the walls – maybe to hide damp patches or something – and odd bowls of cones, and sea-shells; all very interesting but a little untidy. They also had a lovely dog named Mulligan. They reposed in the lounge, awaiting their evening meal, in front of a roaring log fire and really relaxed. The meal was great; cooked by Andrew. They started off with melon decorated with grapes and orange, F had chicken, C and M beef curry all accompanied by rice and a salad consisting of lettuce, broccoli, mushrooms, carrots, green peppers, celery and apple, followed by home-made blackberry ice cream and then coffee. It was all delicious.

They all had a good night but awakened to a very drizzly outlook. They somehow expected a continental-style breakfast, but they had orange juice, cereal, bacon, egg, tomato, mushrooms and fried potato, followed by the usual toast and marmalade. They didn't mention packed lunch feeling they could never cope with anything so mundane! They left their remarks in the visitors' book: 'Delightful and unique in every way, including vittals.' [M didn't know how to spell *vittles* – she does now!] That about summed everything up; only those who have visited Keeper's Cottage would really understand!

Friday (7th). A fond farewell was tendered to all, including Mulligan, and Andrew dropped them back on the path (still raining) and they set off for another day's walking to Monmouth, a distance of about nine miles. Their first good deed for the day was to rescue a sheep lying stiffly on its back with all four legs pointing heavenwards. They thought it was dead, but C advanced towards it and with some difficulty, (as it was lying in a cow pat) rolled it over and away it skipped, apparently none the worse; but for their timely arrival it would surely have died. They got pretty wet but by the time they had had their elevenses the sun shone and their spirits revived. They tramped through fields of cows with abandon.

Their route took them over the River Trothy over which there was supposed to be a footbridge. Unfortunately this did not exist, but there did appear to be logs across the river over which they could walk. C, with determination, placed his boot on the log which proved to be floating, and down he sank into the water below wetting his one leg up to his knee. Unkindly M and F laughed at C who, not bearing any malice, helped them both over without mishap.

Their road eventually took them into a beautiful plantation – Kings Wood – where F and M saw a fallow deer right on their path, but he speedily scampered away at their approach. They climbed up a steep hill and found some nice logs on which to eat their lunch, which consisted of cheese and biscuits, apple and choc. The view from their lunch place was very extensive and spectacular, and the sun shone on them but, of course, it is a well-known adage that 'the sun shines on the righteous'!

They set off at 3.15 p.m. for their walk to Monmouth through more woods and fields. On arrival they had a cup of tea at a Cafe and did not at all appreciate the noise of traffic and seeing people. However it all had to be borne and they then toiled up through the town to the YHA, only to find on arrival, that the key had to be collected from the warden's house a little distance away. C and F went for the key while M remained to mind the haversacks and catch up with these notes. The sun was shining but its rays cast longer and longer shadows until at last it disappeared behind the hills.

As soon as they gained access they registered, purchased

sundries, and made up their beds. There was only one other girl in F and M's dormitory, but she later retired with her husband to a room of their own leaving F and M in sole possession. Poor C as usual, had to share his room with six others and had a somewhat disturbed night. M had to wander along the dim corridor during the night – the door squeaked noisily, but fortunately she did not meet anyone. Both F and M had a good night and arose for breakfast at nine. By that time most of the hostellers had left and they ate their breakfast of cornflakes, and beans on toast in comparative peace. They did their job of cleaning the common room and left the hostel at just after ten o'clock in their light shoes and minus haversacks.

They had difficulty at first keeping on an even course as obviously their haversacks had helped them to balance, but they soon got their walking legs and repaired to the Catholic church to check on the time of Mass the next morning. Had a word with Father O'Brien who obviously had never heard of Offa's Dyke! They did decide that morning to telephone Lieut. Cmdr. Hines at Brockweir to book in for Sunday night and the evening meal. Mrs Hines advised them to take the Wye River alternative route instead of Kymin as it was nicer in every way; this they decided to do as they had a fairly big mileage to cover on Sunday to reach Brockweir. (M was feeling very worried because on phoning Elva she was told that Mitzi was not eating and Elva thought she was pining. This gave M a frightful guilt complex.)

Most of Saturday (the 8th) was spent in buying provisions for their Sunday walk; having morning coffee in style around a table, instead of balancing on a tree trunk or such like, and they had a very nice lunch at the Vine Tavern of chicken for F, ham for

C and M with jacket potatoes followed by chocolate fudge cake for C and F and chocolate ice cream for M, followed by coffee. It was all delicious and they felt quite civilised once more. They seemed quite at a loss to know how to cope with ordinary living, having no route to follow that day, but to-morrow they hoped to be back on the Offa's Dyke Path once more where they so obviously belong. They decided after lunch to go to the museum, but on arrival there F discovered that she had left her camera somewhere – but where? After walking down Monmouth main street for the umpteenth time it was eventually located at their luncheon venue. By this time it was raining and had turned rather cold, so they all trooped into the museum – a very interesting place, mainly relating to Nelson and Lady Hamilton. F and M found a nice comfortable seat and read their papers; after which F did a crossword puzzle and M 'dropped off'.

At about four o'clock C announced that he felt like a cuppa, so they all trooped out to the cafe next door but it was closed. Once again they wandered down the main street, suddenly became fed up, and decided to go back to the hostel, make their own tea and also cook their supper instead of once more having to go down the main street, of which, by this time, they were heartily sick. They purchased bread, mushroom soup and cakes, and returned to the hostel, having collected the key from the warden. On entering the common room they were nearly overcome by a most dreadful smell of Calor gas and it turned out that one of the stoves had been leaking all day. Windows and doors were thrown wide open and the stove was adjusted. C lit the fire, and after their meal F and M had three games of Scrabble, until their eyes could scarcely stay open. They all retired to bed but had rather a disturbed night owing to the local drunks making a disturbance. M arose at seven o'clock because of getting to Mass, and made herself a cuppa. The smell of gas still persisted! After their 'day of rest' one and all were anxious to be on their feet again following the path, but they did feel rested and well able to face their walk to Brockweir.

Sunday (9th). A nice warm morning but rather a heavy drizzle was falling when C and M left for church. By the time the 8.30 Mass was over the weather cleared. They left everything clean and tidy at the hostel and were on their way at 10.15. Once again they wended their way down the main road to what they thought was the Wye Bridge, when M suddenly felt that they were going in the wrong direction so she enquired of a passing gentleman; they were wrong but he put them right and very quickly they were once more on the right road for Redbrook.

For three miles their route took them along the banks of the Wye – most beautiful. They saw swans, ducks and a heron. Rose hips and holly abounded everywhere and it was noticeable what a brilliant red the berries were and so abundant. At Redbrook they left the river and climbed up a very steep flight of steps up into woods. They had their lunch at the edge of the wood reposing on moss-covered boulders; it was a very silent place except for the wind in the trees and the calls of the birds. They had chicken paste and cress rolls, Mars bar and apple. After lunch their way took them along the actual Dyke and then on through Creeping Hill Woods and down on to the road from where they could see Bigsweir Bridge. They took the riverside alternative to Brockweir which was absolutely lovely.

On arrival at Brockweir they could not see Triangle House

so C said that he would walk up the hill to see if he could locate it. M was just enquiring of a youth as to the whereabouts of Triangle House, when who should drive up in their car but Ian and family! M was thrilled to bits to see them but Anne, with tears in her eyes, announced that she had some rather bad news. M's first thought was that something had happened to Monica or Mitzi (their cat) – as if Ian would chase them around all day over Mitzi! But the truth was that they had been burgled! This was tragedy indeed as they were only one day's walk from the end of the path at Chepstow. They felt that they must return as Mrs Pratt had phoned Anne but had not told her the extent of the damage, however the police had advised that they should return. Ian and family had set off from Hereford at about eleven o'clock to try and trace F, C and M and it had taken them until 4.30 to catch up with them, helped along by locals who had kindly phoned around to the bed and breakfast places, which led them eventually to Brockweir. They felt before returning they should contact Lt. Cmdr. and Mrs Hines as they were so near; they turned out to be delightful people. Their evening meal had been prepared for them but they felt they could not spare the time to eat it – by this time M felt physically sick, visualising the house having been ransacked from top to bottom and generally vandalised – but the Hines did give them tea, coffee and jam tarts and they set off, packed like sardines in Ian's car, back to Hereford to pick up Harriet (their car) reposing in Ian's bus garage. It was truly miraculous how the car took all the weight of five adults, the two boys and three very weighty haversacks.

Much phoning was done on reaching Anne's house who generously provided them with food and milk. They eventually set off for Rednal with trepidation wondering what on earth they were going to be confronted with on arrival. Miraculously the damage was not too bad and hardly anything had been stolen with the exception of a small bedside digital clock and C's hand lamp. The upstairs back bedroom, which had housed M's jewellery had not been touched, and the money in the house – about £16.50 in all – was left. The kitchen door, lounge door and office door had all been broken open and new door frames would have to be fitted. The motive for the break-in still remained somewhat of a mystery.

Determined to finish the path down to Chepstow they booked up with Lt. Cmdr. and Mrs Hines for the night of 30th October and hopefully these memoirs would be finished on a happier note.

* * *

The weather during the week preceding the 30th October was so gloriously dry and sunny that panic reigned among C, F and M as they felt sure it could not possibly last! However the forecast was set fair but another crisis arose in the shape of a very bad cold suffered by C. On Friday night, 28th, C felt sure he would not be fit to cope, and F would never know how near M was to phoning her and once more postponing the expedition! Fortunately the next morning, having been dosed with hot lemon and honey, C rallied and decided to risk it. How relieved M was! The warm sunny morning definitely helped too!

The sun shone brilliantly all during the Saturday. M was at the shop and C held the fort while a new kitchen door was fitted, and a further lock placed on the front door, so all being well everything would be safe on their return!

F arrived at about 7.30 p.m. Haversacks were packed and they were all ready to depart at 10.10 the next morning, unfortunately it was rather a cold and gloomy morning but at least dry. After a good journey they arrived at the path in Chepstow, parked Harriet in the Castle Car Park, and set off for Sedbury Cliffs at about 12.15 – a distance of about two miles.

Their route took them alongside a very pungent sewage plant and then into Pennsylvania village actually on the line of the Dyke. They walked along Offa's Close and Mercian Way; also Norse Way. What historical names! Then across fields, passing Buttington Tump earthworks and along a fine stretch of the Dyke to the end of the path on Sedbury Cliffs, arriving there at 1.30 p.m. expecting to have a wonderful and extensive view of the estuary, instead of which there was no view at all as the estuary was hidden by thick shrubbery. However they ate their lunch in the field surrounded by gorse bushes – still in flower – overlooking Chepstow, with the Forest of Dean in the distance. Weather still cloudy but dry. They left at 2.00 p.m. had photographs taken sitting on the Stone marking the end of the path and set off back to the car at Chepstow. They all experienced a slight feeling of anti-climax on reaching the end; what they had expected none of them knew!

They arrived back in Chepstow car park at 3.30 p.m. and went in search of the youth hostel, Catholic church, convent and bus centre. All of them were eventually located but C and M decided to go to their own church at Rednal for the Feast of All Saints at 8.30 p.m. as the convent was too far away. They drove on to Brockweir, through the most beautiful wooded scenery, the leaves just turning into their Autumn glory. *En route* they called in at a very fascinating craft shop at Tintern where they could have spent hundreds of pounds! Instead they purchased one postcard each and M bought Elva's Christmas present of soap!

They received a warm welcome from the Hines and were given a 'cuppa'. Thereafter they had 'the story of her life' narrated by Mrs Hines who was a chain smoker; some of it interesting, some dramatic but otherwise somewhat boring. They came to the conclusion that she was a hypochondriac, apparently suffering from perpetual migraine, but this was not to be wondered at as she never stopped talking. On the other hand she was rather to be pitied as she has no friends, could not drive or walk, and in a place like Brockweir there was nothing else to do!

Dinner was cooked and served by Lieut. Cmdr. Hines and very nice it was too. Shrimps *vol-au-vent* (which poor F couldn't eat as she was allergic to shell-fish), a chicken dish containing ham and mushrooms and some herb which remained a mystery, potato and mixed vegetables, apple pie, ice cream and cream followed later by coffee in the lounge plus further extracts from 'the story of my life', all of which were accompanied by the television which nobody could hear. They retired about 10.30 p.m. and all had a wonderfully comfortable night.

They woke up to a bright and sunny morning – the trees glowed with warmth and colour – and after a very nice breakfast of cornflakes, bacon, egg, fried bread, toast and marmalade they set off for their eight miles to Chepstow. Time 10.10 a.m. They climbed up a terrifically steep hill to get onto the Dyke and the walk thereafter was mainly through woodland paths, part of the Forest of Dean, and far below them they could see the River Wye. They walked on a carpet of golden, red and brown leaves, absolutely enchanting! They stopped for their elevenses sitting on a tree trunk overlooking Tintern Abbey far below, and in the very far distance a view of Hay Bluff. It was difficult to imagine that their walk had taken them all around the Bluff. How on earth had they done it? But they had! They made friends with Sally, a very beautiful black Labrador who was out walking with her master. They continued their walk past the Devil's Pulpit, an outstanding rocky outcrop, again with views of the abbey. On and on, mainly through woods until they eventually arrived at the main road into Chepstow.

They stopped for lunch at the Boughspring Turn, and sat on a conveniently placed bench on the green overlooking the estuary once again, with the Severn Bridge in the distance. Thereafter the walk into Chepstow was uneventful but very pleasant. At one point a most lovely little dog came to greet them bringing his rubber ring for a game, named Rupert, a cross between a terrier and King Charles spaniel. They took the name of the lady who bred them – a Mrs Alastair McGregor of Monmouth, as M decided if ever she could have a dog that would be the type she would like.

Their first port of call on arriving at Chepstow was to the Wye Knot Cafe where they imbibed lots of icy cold orange squash. They were so thirsty it was just like nectar from heaven! They went to look at the cut glass warehouse, and tried to buy a card of the Wye showing the autumn colours, but without success. All this time they had been followed by a Jack-the-Ripper-type of male who tried to cotton on to F by deliberately bumping into her and trying to make conversation, but F and M dived into a shop and eventually got rid of him. Before making their way to the hostel they had a scrumptious meal of haddock and chips for F and M, sausage and chips for C and, full to the brim, they toiled up the very steep hill to the hostel.

This was a beautifully sited hostel overlooking the Severn Bridge and Estuary. They were the only occupants so C and M shared a room leaving F to cope alone in the girls' dormitory, but she said she did not mind. They purchased badges, etc., made up their bunks, and repaired to the common room with 108 miles of Offa's Dyke behind them. Having achieved part of their dream (the southern part) they still had enough enthusiasm to make plans for their assault on the northern part from Prestatyn to Knighton in 1984. They said so many times in amazed unbelief, 'We've done it!' They all played their respective parts in achieving this stupendous action. F in much planning of the route, C escorting them safely over bogs, streams and by-passing bulls, and M in organising the YHA bookings and bed and breakfasts. It was a joint effort, thoroughly enjoyed by one and all – a most worthwhile expedition!

Their last night spent in Chepstow was most comfortable. F and M played two games of Scrabble before retiring to bed, and as they had bottom bunks they lay in their respective bunks looking at the lights on the Severn Bridge and across the Estuary.

On awakening on the morning of 1 November they could not see a thing as a thick mist lay like a pall over the whole landscape. They felt almost glad that their expedition had come to an end, as never would they have found their way through fields and woods in such a mist. Breakfast was eaten, C sprinkling his cornflakes with coffee instead of brown sugar, but he said it gave it quite a tang! They set off for the bus to Brockweir at 9.30 a.m. hoping the driver would be able to find his way! Before leaving the hostel they had quite a long talk with the warden – a Mrs Jordan – who told them the new rules for hostels next year – or lack of them. No lights-out time; in fact it appeared that they were going to be geared to the tastes of the teenagers – not for C, F and M!

They boarded the bus at 10.03 a.m. and on alighting at Brockweir Bridge they had a long and steep hill to walk up to the Hines' house. They viewed with astonishment the route they had taken the day before on their way to Chepstow! How on earth had they done it? An incline of one in three! They were given a welcome drink by Mrs Hines, accompanied by further details of her life and ailments, purchased peppermints from her shop, and set off in Harriet to Hereford, the weather by this time being glorious as the fog had vanished. Stopped for a nice lunch *en route*, called on Anne, and then high-tailed it for home, stopping for water and apples.

They would have plenty of time during the winter months for planning their next trip – hopefully in 1984 – starting from Prestatyn and walking southwards.

Details of approx. expenditure for holiday walking Offa's Dyke from Hay-on-Wye to Chepstow (Sedbury Cliffs) from 3–9 October 1983

	Expenditure		Sub total
3rd October Hay-on-Wye	B&B at Helmont House	£12.00	
	Afternoon tea	£0.58	
	Evening dinner	£3.30	
	Sundry food & drink	£5.66	£21.54
4th October: 8 miles Hay-on-Wye to Capel-y-ffin	Hostel fee	£4.80	
	Supper	£2.80	
	Provisions & badges	£0.78	£8.38
5th October: 11 miles Capel-y-ffin to Pandy	Dinner, B&B at Lancaster Arms		
		£21.60	
	Drinks	£1.00	
	Packed lunches	£2.25	
	Sundries	£0.34	£25.19
6th October: 8 miles Pandy to Llandewi Rhydderch	B&B and evening meal at Julia & Andrew Paxton's	£22.00	
	Sundries	£2.00	£24.00
7th October: 10 miles Llandewi Rhydderch to Monmouth	Hostel fee for two nights	£7.80	
	Supper	£2.60	
	Sundries	£1.19	£11.59
8th October Monmouth	Dinner	£3.30	
	Drinks	£0.67	
	Provisions, coffee, phone	£5.33	£9.30
9th October: 11 miles Monmouth to Brockweir	Drinks	£0.36	
	Phone	£0.10	£0.46
		Total	**£100.46**

By car to Chepstow, walking to Sedbury Cliffs, by car to Brockweir, walking to Chepstow, by bus back to Brockweir from 30 October to 1 November 1983

	Expenditure		Sub-total
30th October: 5 miles To/from Sedbury Cliffs	Coffee Ice cream	£0.60 £0.66	£1.26
31st October: 8 miles Brockweir to Chepstow	B&B and 18.00 evening meal at Triangle House and cancelled meal Hostel fee Food, badges, etc.	£24.00 £5.50 £2.50	£32.00
1st November By bus to Brockweir	Bus fares Lunches Coffee	£1.98 £2.90 £0.60	£5.48
	Total		£38.74
	Total of both trips		£139.20

Total mileage: 61 miles

Third Installment of
Walk along Offa's Dyke
Prestatyn to Welshpool. Very approx. 90 miles

23 June to 3 July 1984

Ever since C, F and M's expedition to Offa's Dyke, M had undergone physiotherapy treatment at Rubery Hospital on her left heel, and they did begin to wonder whether they would ever be able to cope at all in 1984. However, on learning that F had only been able to undertake the walk in 1983 because she took painkillers on account of a very sore foot, M felt thoroughly ashamed of herself and with fierce determination fixed the third stint of their walk on the Dyke for 2 June and the necessary preparations went on apace.

However, after this momentous decision M – always M – succumbed to very bad aches and pains in her legs, and on this occasion decided in her own mind, that they would have to go up by car, F and C walking while M drove from point to point carrying all the luggage. This would have been ideal for C and F to be able to travel minus their heavy packs but not quite so good for M. Eventually the pain drove M to go to see her doctor, who arranged for her to have her joints x-rayed, but in the meantime, equipped her with a goodly supply of painkillers, and told her that walking would do her good, so it looked as though two out of the three would pursue their way 'on drugs'!

F met M at the B.M.I. for a serious discussion about the route, accommodation, etc., using and totally disrupting the peace of the members' room at the B.M.I., but other members there took quite a lively interest in their activities. Fortunately there was a 5 p.m. Mass on Saturdays at Prestatyn, so M phoned a Mrs Tipping and fixed up B&B and E.M. for their first night. The next stay at Rhuallt seemed fairly straightforward with a Mrs Williams, but on phoning Mr Harvey at Llandyrnog matters became a little complicated as he was two miles off the path. They decided that they would avail themselves of his offer of transport. M said airily that they would phone him on nearing Llandyrnog but Mr Harvey said they could not do that as there was no phone! On enquiring their ages he somehow worked out that they would arrive at London Bridge Car Park about 5 p.m. – wherever that was – so that was how matters were left. They were to look out for a white car. They all sincerely hoped that they would meet up with Mr Harvey, as the meeting place was obviously in the middle of nowhere, but it all sounded delightfully vague. Here's hoping!

By the 27 May M became steadily more stiff and immobile and decided to visit the doctor once more regarding x-rays, etc., but she did begin to feel that she could not cope with walking. Naturally this put them all in a dreadful dilemma. Should they postpone the trip in the hope that M would recover, or should they go by car with M meeting them each evening? Why on earth couldn't things be straight forward for a change? Anyway the doctor said that they would have to postpone their holiday, so after lengthy discussions with F they decided on 23 June. Much phoning ensued regarding bookings but things were eventually settled to everybody's satisfaction, as all ladies were prepared to change the date so all was set for 23 June hopefully – a miracle indeed! All during the night before they should have originally started, the heavens opened, and the days following were very wet and unsettled, although interspersed with warm sunshine. Perhaps M's indisposition was for the best after all – only time would tell.

Saturday 23 June dawned bright and sunny, and at 10.15 a.m. C and M waited in Digbeth Station for F, already having consumed Mars and Bounty bars, owing to starvation having set in on account of their very early breakfast. F duly arrived, they boarded the coach, and the journey up to Prestatyn was fairly uneventful. M sat next to a very interesting young man named Ken, who was walking all around Snowdonia. M advised him to strike inland at Llanbedr and over the Roman Steps and the Rhinogs to Dolgelly, and then over Cader, and he did say he would like to do that.

On arrival at Prestatyn F, C and M literally staggered from the coach into a Cafe for a cuppa which was really welcome. They then repaired to 112 Marine Road where they were made very welcome, unpacked, ate the remainder of their lunch, and set off to explore Prestatyn. A very nice clean town with lovely shops, but no postcards of Offa's Dyke. C and M went to the five o'clock Mass, and later met F back at Mrs Tipping's for a really lovely meal of soup, chops, potatoes, cauliflower, peas and mint sauce, followed by strawberry flan and cream, tea and coffee. It did start to rain a little but that did not deter them from meandering to the beginning of the path on the sea-front where the tide was full in. They walked about 1½ miles along the Promenade; the waves thundered against the stones and until they turned to go back and faced into the rain they had not realised how really wet it was. An ominous start indeed! Their wet clothes were handed over to Mrs Tipping for drying. Rather a bad beginning, the weather report forecasting more wet weather to follow!

However on Sunday 24 June, they awoke to sunshine and their spirits immediately soared. Their lunch was prepared in the bedroom, and breakfast taken at 8.30 – the usual bacon, sausage, fried bread, etc., all very nice and they set off at 9.45, C and M protected by plastic bags inside their boots. Just as well to be prepared for torrential rain! However, no rain did fall upon them and the weather was nice and dry with a fresh wind – at their backs.

They climbed out of Prestatyn puffing and blowing – obviously out of condition – and on arrival at some crossroads were plainly looking bewildered and lost, when a plaintiff voice said 'Can I help you'? Quite clearly this lady, who had come from London (Nancy they called her) was all set for a chat, and invited them in for coffee, but C, F and M really hadn't got time – and in view of later events it was a blessing they did not dally – and so kindly refused.

They continued to climb onwards and upwards and came to a point where the Offa's Dyke sign seemed to point right, but the notes said left. F was persuaded, against her better judgment, to go right but after at least a mile of steep climbing up a very narrow difficult path both, F and M wanted to retrace their steps, but C airily said that they would come out at the same place anyway! M, feeling that C was always right, meekly followed – F really had to – but eventually M, feeling in her bones that they were wrong, became adamant and said that she was going back. C turned round with muttered curses, unable to abandon F and M to their own devices, but it certainly was a good thing that they did as they were completely on the wrong route. C completely lost the confidence of F and M at this juncture!

Catching up with the memoirs; just above Prestatyn

Eventually at 12.15 they arrived back at the aforementioned signpost, and started off once more in the correct direction, actually making very good time. It took them ages to actually get out of sight of Prestatyn; F and M kept bidding farewell to the sea feeling sure that they had seen the last of it, but it kept coming back into view again. They had their lunch – cheese and cucumber sandwiches – sitting on stones and logs in a lovely field, but they did not linger very long as the wind was a bit chilly.

M stopped at many houses asking to have her flask filled with cold water, and it was always kindly given to her. M developed a terrible thirst, possibly due to the tablets, and she did not find the stiles very easy to negotiate as there were certainly lots and lots of them.

At about 3.45 they stopped at Bodlonfa to have a cup of tea. F doled out mint cake and C and M divested themselves of their plastic bags as they had walked them into holes, and their feet were sodden with perspiration – almost worse than being wet through with rain! On the path F and M had a most difficult stile to negotiate, which they actually had to climb on their knees, and having completed this exercise discovered they had been watched all the time by a farmer who seemed highly amused; F and M felt quite embarrassed! The sun continued to shine brilliantly and the views of the mountains and valleys all around were glorious.

By 4.30 they were making their final descent into Rhuallt which was terrifically steep, through a beautiful wood lined with ferns, foxgloves – and brambles. On reaching the main A55 they just sank onto a wayside seat, too tired to move, and contemplated the very heavy traffic which really disturbed them after the peace of the hills. At length they realised that if they didn't move they probably wouldn't be able to, if they sat there much longer, so C enquired the whereabouts of Mrs Williams of Pant Ifan and was told that it was the last farm on the left about a mile away. It would be!

They gathered all their strength and will-power for the trek, but fortunately it was only about half a mile, and on arrival they just collapsed into their rooms utterly exhausted. What C, F and M do for pleasure! But it was the challenge of completing the Offa's Dyke path that egged them on and kept them going. F's room was on the ground floor, and how C and M envied her not having to climb the stairs; even the bathroom was on the ground floor so F really had it made. M did wonder how she would manage during the night wandering about in the dark – that remained to be seen. The house was an interesting old farmhouse full of beautiful antiques. They went out for their meal to the White House Inn at Rhuallt – only a few minutes away thank goodness – where they had chicken and ham pie, chips, potatoes, carrots and peas followed by strawberry gâteau for F, peach melba for C and M, plus coffee and tea, all very nice. They returned to Pant Ifan feeling gloriously well-fed and contented with life despite their aching limbs and weak legs!

Much in this farmhouse was very beautiful but definitely the worse for wear. C sat on a chair to take his well-earned rest which immediately collapsed beneath him – very typical actually. Many latches were broken on doors, things held together by string – pretty chaotic in fact but with it all a homely and happy atmosphere pervaded. C and M slept like logs between purple sheets and blankets, F between yellow.

At 8.15 C, F and M descended (not F of course as she was already downstairs) to breakfast. From the smells rising from the kitchen it seemed it would be good, and it was. Cornflakes and Weetabix, bacon, tomato, fried bread and egg, toast and marmalade. The two pussies called in to see them, and fought over the bacon rind, each holding an end and tugging. The kitten – Spot – usually won. Spot was covered with stripes but apparently when she was born she did have an orange spot on her forehead – hence her name they supposed. Weather cloudy but fine and forecast good. They phoned Kenneth to confirm Monday evening rendezvous at London Bridge car park.

They set off at 9.50 (24 June), full once again of life and enthusiasm for the day before them. Elevenses were taken at the side of the lane near Sodom. The path was clearly marked until the notes said 'Left' which turn they took and descended three quarters of a mile down a very steep and winding lane. At the bottom they enquired of a tractor driver only to find they should not have turned left after all but right! Back they toiled, amidst many murmurings and grumblings, and started off again. The walk was very beautiful, with magnificent views, but the descent into Bodfari was quite traumatic – extremely steep and very overgrown with nettles, brambles, etc. At the bottom of the hill the door of the Downing Arms was open to greet them, and they literally fell on to the seat in front and gulped their drinks with relish.

The walk after lunch was very lovely – actually the commencement of the Clwydian Range – a range of heights of striking and varied outline, twenty-two miles long with nine summits over a thousand-feet high. From the top they could see the whole length of the Snowdon Range, round to Llandudno, Rhyl and Prestatyn and the Dee Estuary. The path over Moel Y Parc was not very clear but eventually they found it and arrived at Clwyd Llangwfan car park just before 5.30 p.m. Just prior to their arrival there they met the only walker they had seen all day, who was from the Continent, and who had been walking from south to north. He had come through very rainy weather with mist on the mountain which had obliterated all views. C, F and M came to the conclusion that they were lucky to be travelling from north to south as they had had no rain ever since leaving Prestatyn, and the wind had been behind them the whole of the way.

Kenneth duly turned up on time, and they motored in luxury the three miles to his home – absolute heaven to be off their feet for a while and minus the weight of their packs; although they did view with great concern the very steep climb which had to be negotiated the next morning; however, sufficient unto the day . . .

On arrival at Gwenallt Llandyrnog they received a tumultuous welcome from Jessica – a six-month-old puppy and three lovely cats – Kerry, Sheba and Bruno. Bruno the lady and Sheba the Tom! The vagaries of Welsh farmhouses! C and M were on the ground floor this time but, of course, the bathroom was upstairs! F was bang next door to this once more – her luck!

In due time they were presented with an enormous meal – lettuce soup (rather insipid), fish with a very nice sauce, and then *pie*. F thought that it was beef but from the beginning M was highly suspicious and did wonder whether it was horse as she couldn't think of anything else of a like texture. C and F ate theirs with relish, but fortunately for M Jessica came in and relieved her of most of it for which she was very thankful. The mystery was eventually solved and the dish was hare; this was later confirmed by Mr Harvey who obviously had shot it and C nearly swallowed the lead shot to prove it! Mr Harvey was obviously older than his wife; he had been retired for eight years and gloried in doing the cooking. He loved messing about with exotic dishes which his wife never appreciated. No wonder! She was a nurse working on nights and was pretty unhappy, living as isolated as she was, particularly as she could not drive and was dependent on Kenneth taking her into the hospital; and apparently he was not always very willing. F and M were able to swipe some bread off the table for their mid-day meal next day – very useful this as they would not be passing through any villages whatsoever. No purchases of cards or anything else had so far been made, as no shops had been sighted.

They retired to C and M's room after dinner but all the chairs were occupied by the animals, so they stretched out on their beds and had a rest, prior to visiting the Kimmel Arms Tavern in the village. C had two lagers and lime, F and M the usual lime and lemon. On their return to Gwenallt C and M found their bedroom was like a hothouse and they were concerned that not one window could be opened, not conducive to waking up fresh and lively in the morning. They wandered around until about 2.30 a.m. but thereafter did manage to sleep a bit. They woke up to a lovely sunny day and the wind had dropped. C had a slight attack of *petit mal* but Mrs Harvey said it certainly was slight, however M was worried all day!

At 9.50 Kenneth took them back to London Bridge car park ready for the very steep climb up Moel Arthur, and to the summit of the Clwydians (1,820 ft.). Amazingly – and quite contrary to the early morning promise – they were soon shrouded in mist and it poured. Out came their kagoules, leggings, rain hoods, etc., amidst much muttering, and they plodded onwards and steadily upwards without seeing a thing in front or behind! Eventually they dropped down to a car park the other side of Moel Arthur, and there met a young man, covered in tattoos, who was walking to Prestatyn that night! What it was to be young! He had come over the proper Offa's Dyke path and said how very tough the going had been – quite contrary to the written instructions. C, F and M took the gentler path, and for most of the rest of that day – until at least 4.00 p.m. – wished they hadn't, as they got miles out of their way and hopelessly lost.

They made one or two enquiries of farmers in the village of Cilcain and were directed up Moel Fawr. A few purchases were made at the P.O. and drinks quaffed at the White Horse Inn. Once again they asked the way, which agreed with the directions they had been previously given, but they were hell bent on finding the proper Offa's Dyke path – or was it only C? – so did not take the advice given. They wandered all day in the Clwydians, and eventually sat down by a very pretty stream for their lunch at about 2.00 p.m. feeling very tired, frustrated and somewhat worried as they had no idea where they were. Bread taken from Mr Harvey, and ham torn by hand, was proffered by M to F and C, and it tasted scrumptious and was eaten with relish. After this repast they were still undecided as to their route. C wanted to go straight up and over Moel Famau but F and M felt they had had enough, so they opted to go around the mountain instead. This put an extra mile or two on their journey but eventually, about 4.30, they came upon Jubilee Tower and the right path – at last! C's brilliant leadership and sense of direction, at this juncture, restored F and M's confidence in C!

In their relief at once more being on the path they decided that they had time to stop for a cuppa and biscuits, but their peace was somewhat shattered by a hurricane or tornado which looked as though it was going to dive bomb them. However, the danger passed, and they just sat and stared at the wonderful view stretching from the sea, the Snowdon Range, the Rhinogs, Cader Idris and beyond. It was truly magnificent and words could not possibly describe it.

They then descended to their place of abode, Mrs Hughes, Carneddi, Llanbedr Hall Drive. This turned out to be a most

Dropping down to Carneddi

glorious house set upon a hill. F was given the daughter's bedroom while C and M occupied the caravan outside. This was small but extremely cosy. Mr Hughes was a civil engineer which explained the beautiful layout of the house and garden. C, F and M eventually organised themselves, washed and changed – not that they had very much choice to change into – and then made their way to the Griffin Hotel. They consumed asparagus quiche and salad, strawberries and cream followed by coffee – really scrumptious. Very interesting company too – a television camera man, an animated girl – very made up – who looked like an actress, and other out-of-the-ordinary individuals.

After their meal they went for a short walk and then to bed. C and M had a really warm comfortable night in the caravan, and thoroughly enjoyed the novelty of it all, despite the fact that they did have to wander through the garden during the night to their own 'private' bathroom at about 4 a.m. As usual F had the privilege of one 'next door'! C and M sometimes felt quite deprived on that score! The day dawned bright and sunny. There were two cats and a dog living with the family, Poppett and Kissy the cats, and a golden retriever.

On arrival the previous night at their setting-off point, the next morning they had been so appalled at the climb back to the car park – about two miles steeply winding up all the way – that they felt never could they accomplish it even at the beginning of the day! So M enquired of Mrs Williams whether she knew of anybody who could take them up by car. As M had been hoping, she offered to take them herself for which they were all so grateful, and were then able to enjoy their breakfast of orange juice, cereal, bacon, egg, sausage, tomato, toast and marmalade, feeling that they would be starting their climb up the very steep path up Moel Fenlli, feeling fresh and on top of the morning!

The path really was like going up the side of a house – they went up, almost on their knees, clinging to the wire fence on their left, and down the other side on their seats! *En route* one renowned crotchety farmer had diverted the path, but actually,

F, C and M were truly thankful, as it saved them climbing Moel
Eithinen and down the other side – they just went round it. That
morning they had their 'elevenses' at the respectable hour of
11.30 a.m. – a most unusual occurrence for them.

On arrival at the Clwyd Gate Inn at 12.30, they discovered
that ramblers were requested to remove hiking boots, so they
padded in in their stocking feet and partook of three coffees in
the sun lounge, overlooking miles of beautiful scenery, although
it did look a little like rain. It was almost a waste of words to
attempt a description of the scenery. They appreciated the luxury
of walking along a beautiful carpet patterned with roses to
the pink-tiled toilet – very different from their usual decor of
brambles, stinging nettles, etc., with the accompanying hazards
to the person!

Their route took them around the west flank of Moel Gyw
from where they had a clear view of Ruthin and the Clwydians.
They had their lunch at 2.30 p.m. overlooking a col at Garreg
Llwyd and just as they finished it did begin to rain – a thin
drizzling rain which somewhat damped their spirits – and
clothing. The mist descended and it was a little eerie but as
they wended their way downhill they soon dropped below the
mist. They had to negotiate two fields containing some very
large fierce-looking bullocks, but as they could not deviate they
pressed on regardless, M breathing a prayer for a safe passage!
Through one field a little lamb pranced up to C looking for
some fuss and it allowed them to stroke it. It was a sweet
little thing and did follow them for quite a long way bleating
piteously. They stopped for afternoon tea at 4.30 feeling in
need of sustenance after negotiating the cattle! This had been

their very first encounter and they hoped it would be their last! By this time the weather had greatly improved and the wind was at their backs as it had been every day. This was a blessing because at times it had been quite strong and boisterous.

On arrival at Llandegla Village they enquired as to where Mrs Callaghan of The Bryn lived, and were told it was a further half mile up a very steep hill. Oh dear! Anyhow, on arrival all was worthwhile. Their rooms were beautiful, each with its own washbasin, electric kettle for making tea or coffee and home-made cake. They all had a good wash and swiped some of the delicious cake for their meal on the next day! After cleaning up they went down to The Plough for their much-needed evening meal. Their meal consisted of quiche salad, strawberries and cream for C and F but M couldn't decide whether to have coffee meringue or meringue surprise. On enquiring of the waiter what the surprise meringue was he said that it was a surprise. She asked for that of course, and couldn't resist it and it was delicious – a bit of everything but she was never quite sure what!

They went for a short walk before going in and then straight to their beds – luxury indeed. They made their own drinks in the bedroom and just wallowed. They awoke to the sound of mooing cows and bleating sheep – rather a misty outlook but nice and mild. They felt that they had rather a long and arduous day before them, so had asked for breakfast at eight o'clock instead of their usual 8.30 a.m. Lovely breakfast of fruit juice (prunes for C), bacon, scrambled egg, tomato and fried bread, all arranged on the plates in a very artistic fashion by Mrs Callaghan. She was a very talented lady and much of her handiwork was displayed around her house. C managed to sprinkle his All Bran with salt instead of sugar, but after mixing it with three lumps of sugar he said it tasted all right!

They set off at 9.10 a.m. (in rain and mist by this time) up through a thickly wooded forest of pines. It was very hot as they were wearing their cagoules, etc., and there was not a breath of wind in the forest. Eventually they came out on Llandegla Moor, the country becoming wilder, in fact very bleak indeed – and more eerie with mist swirling all around. F and M breathed a prayer that all would be well and, as usual, it was and they reached the other side in safety, although it was a somewhat uncanny experience. Their path then took them through further pine woods (the song of the cuckoo abounding) and eventually on to a narrow ledge around Eglwyseg Crags for about two and a half miles with extensive views of the mountains all around them, and the Eglwyseg River flowing below them in the valley.

After lunch their path took them along Precipice Walk – by that time the sun was shining brilliantly and, of course, they were too hot! In fact, while stopping for a drink at the side of the road, M changed her blouse for a thinner one regardless of any passing traffic. They were all quite abandoned now! From this road fine views could be seen of Llangollen and the Dee Valley.

It seemed rather a long three miles but at length they dropped gradually down through lovely woods where only the sound of twittering birds could be heard – to Trevor, and found Mrs Humphreys of Oaklands just on the main road. They were thankful to arrive, after walking about ten and a half miles of fairly arduous terrain but that day they had not been lost once – a great improvement!

They did not feel at all 'right' in a town but Mrs Humphreys made them welcome with a cuppa and it was a nice comfortable house, but they felt that they definitely preferred the old farmhouses. For their evening meal they had soup, roast lamb, potatoes, carrots and cauliflower, pear flan and coffee. They managed to buy their first cards of the holiday from the P.O. opposite. Had a quiet evening watching television and went to bed with a lovely cup of hot chocolate inside them; tea for C.

Usual breakfast of orange juice, All Bran flakes, bacon, sausage, tomato, etc. They were enjoying themselves so much that they began to wonder whether they could return home later than planned, but as this would have necessitated C getting another prescription for tablets, they decided that they would have to locate a doctor if they wanted to extend their holiday – and perhaps get to Knighton! Happy thought indeed!

Friday 29th. Their route to Chirk took them over the swing bridge – Telford's Pontcysyllte Aqueduct. They rather dreaded that as they had been told of some rather scary experiences regarding wind catching the haversacks and dangerously swaying the owners! However, there wasn't much wind, and they crossed it safely, although viewing the River Dee far below was a bit frightening. F completely overcame her fear to such an extent that she actually balanced herself and took two photographs whilst crossing it! Well done F. Their way then lead them along the Llangollen Canal and the working of a swing bridge over the canal was demonstrated to them by two very pleasant girls who were given 10p each for their trouble, although this was in no way expected. Elevenses were consumed actually on the northernmost part of the Dyke and photographs were taken.

They wended their way onwards towards Chirk Castle only

to find that it was closed that day. Anyway they had their picnic lunch in a nearby field where there were dozens and dozens of rabbits scampering about. On to Chirk then to find Mrs Williams and her Georgian bungalow! At first they went right past it, but were eventually directed correctly and it turned out to be very nice and called Dunroamin. Mrs Williams used to live in Boldmere but was now sadly widowed and obviously very lonely. Everything very luxurious – as usual! C and M would definitely not take kindly to going back to 165! The same for F no doubt!

Having washed and endeavoured to look respectable for 'town' life, they went in search of a surgery for C's prescription – M decided to ask for more of her tablets as well. They easily found one and had to call for them the next morning. F and M, as they walked through Chirk amongst the smart and well-dressed citizens, suddenly decided they must visit a hairdresser. They rushed into a likely-looking salon and impetuously made an appointment for 5.30 that afternoon. In the meantime, all being consumed with thirst, they went into a café and drank oodles of tea and coffee. At the appointed hour F and M entered the salon. M went first, and a very competent-looking female attacked M's hair with gusto and her greying locks fell all around her on the floor. M felt a little perturbed as she did not have much hair to start with! F was treated likewise, and they each thought it would be about £1.00, but to their dismay it was £1.50 and they both hoped they looked better for the exercise.

After this F and M walked along the viaduct looking for C, and met five ladies on a barge who had just spent rather a miserable holiday on the canal travelling from Trevor to Chester and back, but their weather had not been very good. By this time the sun was shining brilliantly. C and M took themselves off to 7 p.m. Mass as it was the Feast of St Peter and Paul, while F busied herself phoning for their next overnight accommodation. They all met up after Mass for their meal at the Hand Hotel. Cheshire pie for C and M, plaice and chips for F followed by orange cheesecake and coffee – all very nice. Booked for Sunday night at Llanymynech – Saturday booked at Carreg-y-Big Farm, actually on the Dyke. They all retired to bed about 10.00 p.m. for a really early night. Slept the sleep of the just and breakfasted at 8.15 a.m. Into Chirk to collect tablets for C and M. M, trying to be helpful, gave the chemist her old bottle containing some tablets, to save another bottle, but either by accident or design he removed her old tablets, put the new ones in, and she then had less than she started with!

They set off once more from Chirk at about 9.30 a.m. and had what seemed a very long two-mile walk along the road. When they branched off the road they had a terrific hill to climb and it was very warm and close. Fortunately they passed one isolated cottage where the lady gave them cold spring water to drink and filled their water bottles. How lovely and refreshing that was! This lady and her husband turned out to be from Birmingham, where they had lived in police quarters – the husband being an inspector – at Hay Mills, Small Heath and Sparkhill. They had retired to that beautiful cottage above Chirk overlooking the castle, and were indeed very happy enjoying the peace and quiet.

Still climbing steeply they stopped for elevenses right on the dyke itself. Over fields, up and down. They stopped for lunch on a high plateau – sort of common land. They then dropped down through fields and woods to Carreg-y-big Farm arriving at about

2.45 p.m. Mrs Jones gave them a warm welcome. They washed and changed ready to be taken to Oswestry for the 4.30 Saturday Mass. They arranged also to be fetched back – a blessing indeed!

They wandered around Oswestry but none of them liked it; a very messy place and they were not at all impressed; they had definitely completely outgrown towns and the accompanying crowds. Sat in the park for a while until it was time for Mass. F went off into the town to do the shopping and C and M met her again in the park after the service. They went into a cafe for a cuppa but the longer they lingered in Oswestry the crumbier it seemed to become.

At the appointed time they draped themselves on the fire station wall to meet Mr Jones who was collecting them at 6.30. How dire it would have been had they had to walk all the way back to the farm from Oswestry – three miles by road up a very steep hill. As soon as they arrived at the farm, dinner was served. Tomato soup, gammon, potatoes and cauliflower, rhubarb tart and custard, tea – all very nice. Mr and Mrs Jones had three sons and two daughters – three married, two at home. Very untidy by the look of their bedrooms too! Carreg-y-Bin was a lovely old farmhouse with beams, etc., but everything on the squiff from pictures to furniture! The Jones went out for the evening and left C, F and M in charge. They gave the impression of being an immensely happy carefree family but a little happy-go-lucky and somewhat 'messy'. F and M coped with the washing-up in the somewhat haphazard kitchen! That evening a long time was spent planning their route as F and M did not really want to return to Birmingham – *ever* – certainly not before Thursday, but definite plans had not been settled.

On the Sunday they woke up to glorious sunshine. Breakfast was served – grapefruit juice, bacon, egg, sausage and tomato, etc. M went to say good-bye to the calves and had quite a chat with Mrs Jones about the W.I., and they started on their way at about 9.30 a.m. A mile up the road took them to the Old Oswestry Racecourse, where they met an old gentleman sunning himself who had been born in Oswestry, and he told them that it wasn't really a racecourse as such, but the Welsh used to bring their horses and trade there.

On they went along the actual Dyke, through woods, glorious smell of honeysuckle, elder, etc. Butterflies, moths and bees buzzed and flew around all over the place. Absolutely enchanting. Their path dropped down to the Old Mill Inn where they had a most welcome drink – although the inn was not officially open. Up they climbed towards Moelydd Hill where they got hopelessly and completely lost. The signposting was quite incorrect and had they not met a gentleman in a car who directed them, they would have gone miles out of their way.

They stopped for lunch on the lower slopes of Moelydd – corned beef sandwiches, Eccles cakes, chocs and peaches – and had a lovely rest for about an hour.

At this juncture C discovered that he had left his pills at Carreg-y-big – after all the trouble of getting a further supply! A return on the following Tuesday now looked inevitable. Again, owing to wrong signposting, they got lost but as they dropped down through very steep woods to a house, a lady heard them talking, gathered that they were lost, and told them to call at her house. She was so nice and soon put them on their proper route, which meant by the time they had finished with Moelydd, they had been all the way round it and up and down twice.

On they went towards Llanymynech Hill; here again they wandered off the path, which was very poorly signposted, so in desperation M called at a deserted looking farmhouse hoping to get directions. The farmer's wife eventually put in an appearance

Looking back at Llanmynech from whence they had just come!

and they found that they were not too far off the right path. When they reached the summit of Llanmynech Hill they stopped for a cuppa with views right over the Shropshire Plain stretching out below them. When the sun had sunk down a little and it was cooler they continued the final trek into Llanmynech – a very steep descent through woods. C kept plunging down into the undergrowth declaring that he was on the right path, but this time F and M were adamant and stood their ground firmly, until C discovered his mistake and came clambering up again.

Through losing their way they had covered twelve and a half miles that day under rather hot conditions, and they arrived at The Lion at 7.15 p.m. feeling rather exhausted, with just enough strength to climb up to their rooms and collapse on their beds. M had been feeling rather worried because a farmer had walked beside her into Llanmynech and asked where they were staying. M said The Lion and there was rather a strained silence. M asked why and he simply answered that he never went in there himself as he much preferred the other inn. However, on arrival it didn't look too bad; in any case they could all have fallen asleep in a cow-shed they felt so tired. The evening meal was quite good; F had chicken and chips with peas; M, steak and kidney pie, chips and peas; and C, ham salad followed by peach melba.

Incidentally on their actual arrival at The Lion, the proprietor had said to C, 'Are you the gentleman from Carreg-y-big who left some pills behind?' Mrs Jones had travelled all the way to The Lion to deliver them for C which was kindness indeed. In past days Queen Victoria had slept at the inn which was half in England and half in Wales. They all had a very good night followed by breakfast at 8.30 a.m.

It became quite obvious at this point that they would not be able to finish the path this time, as they could only return home to Birmingham from Welshpool or Knighton, on account of the transport difficulties. They decided to return by public transport of some sort from Welshpool, and set off for their last night's stay at Pool Quay. Another beautiful day, the sun shining, with only about seven miles in front of them – unless they got lost of course! After drawing their pensions in the village they were on the road once more at 10.15 a.m. Their way took them along the Shropshire Grand Union Canal which was a far pleasanter diversion than along the main road which was the official path, although one and a half miles further – but what was a mere one and a half miles to them now?

There was much to see along the canal: ducks, swans with cygnets, kingcups, dragonflies galore, moths of quite uncommon species and wild flowers of all kinds. As usual they were in too much of a hurry to leave the tow-path, but again they were looked after as at the precise moment they started to leave the canal two people came along who were walking northwards and put them right! Despite the fact that both C and F had Ordnance Surveys – and could actually read them – the maps never seem to be consulted at the crucial moment; consequently the errors in navigation! M, of course, who could hardly read a map anyway, never quite knowing exactly where she was, was completely exonerated!

They called in at the Golden Lion for their usual lime and lemon and lager and set off once more at noon in sunshine but with a nice cool breeze. The going was rather tedious along the Severn flood bank, but at least it was flat, although it stretched for miles. They had lunch on the bank, chicken and ham paste, Mars bars and apples. A little further on they sat on the embankment by the upper reaches of the Severn for half an hour as they had made good time. On again at 3.45 p.m., arriving at Pool Quay at 4.45 p.m. They stopped for a cuppa – whatever would they have done without their flasks and cuppas – and then wended their way to the Powys Arms, which turned out to be a lovely

old inn run by two rather old-maidish types and one elderly
gentleman, or so it seemed. Later this supposition was proved to
be quite wrong, as the inn was run by a Mr and Mrs Charnock
– a Lancashire couple – and the other rather old-fashioned lady
was a local widow who used to help. It was all very charming
and old-worldy.

Another young man from Stoke arrived and pitched his tent
on the lawn for the night. He was walking to Trevor the next day
– C, F and M had stayed there three nights previously! He really
looked tough. Their evening meal was very nice – mushroom
soup, steak, chips, cauliflower and carrots followed by nectarines
and ice cream plus tea. They watched *Coronation Street* on the
television which made them realise they were about to re-enter
into their old familiar world, and then went for a stroll. Back to
F's room for a brew-up of hot chocolate and so to bed.

Everything in the Powys Arms sloped; floors, windows,
ceilings, furniture and walls, but with it all it was really charming
and they all fell in love with it. Had a good night, followed by
a breakfast of bacon, egg, sausage, beans and liver. They did
eventually get a drink but there seemed to be some confusion
regarding cups, and the serving lady kept flitting between the
tables filching odd cups, but all was well in the end. Sadly they
left about 9.30 a.m. for Welshpool and home, hoping to return
in October to actually walk from Pool Quay to Knighton and
finish the Dyke, and so win their badges! Only another twenty-
eight miles or so to do!

They set off along the tow-path in glorious sunshine passing a
Swannery Breeding Enclosure where all kinds of strange-looking
swans were swimming around. Some all black, some black with

white underneath their wings, and others of various colours. They stopped for their elevenses on the tow-path and were joined by a lovely little dog who helped them to eat their biscuits – Bonzo of Buttington – or so they named him.

Eventually they arrived at Welshpool feeling quite depressed by the sight of traffic, crowds, the proverbial litter, and shops. They enquired the times of the buses, which did not fit in too well, and then meandered slowly through the congested streets to the station, to enquire times of trains, not really caring whether there was one or not. Just as they arrived at the station a train drew in and they were told that it was the one they wanted. Without hesitation – or even tickets – they all bundled in, not really being quite sure where it was going, or what the fare was or even if they had enough money. However it was going to Shrewsbury and Wolverhampton so all was well.

They drew into Wolverhampton at 1.15 having had a bit of lunch on the train. They had to catch a slow train to Birmingham, and the sight of the Black Country and its hideous factories and housing estates really saddened them, but at least they were thankful that they did not have to live amongst it all. So there they were again – at the end of their fourth attempt to finish the Dyke, still with the anticipation of a further twenty-eight miles to go. But anticipation lasts longer, the enfolding is more gradual and therefore more satisfactory. So they were looking forward to their final trip in October!

Last Installment of Offa's Dyke Walk
Buttington to Lower Spoad. Approx. 21 miles.

27–31 October 1985

By October 1984 all thoughts of completing the Dyke that year were banished from C, F and M's minds as M's polymyalgia made it impossible to even contemplate, so some time in 1985 was vaguely fixed upon.

By April 1985 M began to feel that she would not be able to cope ever; when she suddenly decided to go on a ramble with the church group, and found that, bolstered up by steroids and painkillers, she could cover six to seven miles at a fairly slow pace. Once more their thoughts turned towards completing walking Offa's Dyke that year, and after the church ramble to Chaddesley Corbett Blue woods on 27 May, they all sprang into action and started to make definite plans. Accommodation addresses and route maps were carefully studied, and 21 September was tentatively fixed for their starting date. F undertook to map out the route so things really began to move once more.

A fierce determination gripped all three of them to finish the Dyke by the end of 1985. Poor F's feet were giving her trouble and she was on painkillers; so too M; and C was taking drugs for his *petit mal*, so all three of them were depending on drugs of some sort to get them to Lower Spoad, but this in no way deterred them. At this stage Anne requested they should take Martin with them and they agreed to this, provided that the necessary accommodation would be available; he was a great walker and very enthusiastic.

Eventually Sunday 29 September was the date agreed for their departure, and M was able to book at the four chosen addresses so all was settled – or so they thought! Once again calamity struck! F broke her ankle getting off a bus on 6 August and so all plans for 29 September had to be abandoned. After much consultation it was decided to try to start on 27 October, in the fond hope that F's ankle would be sufficiently well for her to cope. All accommodation was fortunately re-booked for those dates. Although the weather had been pretty bad for the summer of 1985, a glorious spell of really hot weather from the middle of September onwards was enjoyed. Could it possibly last for them they wondered!

On Tuesday 22 October, Miriam, who was staying with them, took them in her car to spy out some of the route. All told they travelled about 165 miles that day, and located Newcastle Hall and The Drewin, two of the addresses where they intended staying. They had a most interesting trip and espied with trepidation the hills they would have to encounter on their walk. Arrangements were made to meet Ian and family in the car park at Clun at 11 a.m. on Sunday, 27 October, for the beginning of their final onslaught on Offa's Dyke.

The first setback occurred when Anne phoned to say that Martin had a dreadful cough and she did not think that he was fit enough to go as he had coughed all night. Poor Martin so often seemed to be ill and his activities had to be cancelled. However, the arrangement to meet them at Clun still held.

The usual conferences took place as to what they should carry and what they should not, and much packing and unpacking ensued. F duly arrived at 165 on the Saturday. C put all clocks back one hour and intended to have an early night, but this did not materialise as he watched the snooker semi-final. However by 8.39 a.m. on the 27 October, after fond farewells to poor little Mitzi, they set off, the weather being calm and still. It was rather misty so views were not very clear; still it was dry which, when embarking on such a trip as this, was always a great blessing and mattered most.

They stopped at Craven Arms for C to stock up with tobacco, and on to Clun where the Cook clan were waiting for them at 10.15 a.m. They all drove to Newcastle Hall – their last port of call – where they had had permission to park Harriet for a few days in the farmyard. Then they all piled into Ian's car for the journey to Buttington – a distance of about twenty miles. Martin and James were jammed in the dog compartment with Gemma, while C, F and M sat in the back clutching their haversacks. Eventually they arrived at their starting point near Stonehouse (the signpost pointed to Hope – most appropriate they thought), and after coffee and biscuits, they bade farewell to Ian, Anne and the boys, and Gemma of course, and wended their way very steeply uphill to Beacon Ring at a height of 1,400 feet having climbed for about two miles.

Crossing one field C heard the pounding of hooves and thinking that it was a horse-rider looked round and was confronted by a very frisky pony who was all set for a game. It began to chase

C, and F, and M, seeing what was happening, quickly made for the stile to get out of the way. F and M safely negotiated the stile, but C literally collapsed over it, and fell on to the ground on the other side. He quickly recovered though, and they made their way to the ramparts of Beacon Ring where they had their lunch. It was rather chilly sitting still, so they did not tarry for long. The view would have been glorious on a clear day, but as it was the landscape faded away into the haze of the far distance.

Their path led them through fields and on into Leighton Woods. The hush of the countryside was over all, the only sound being the leaves of the trees rustling and falling on to the ground in the slight breeze, like the sea on a shingle beach. By this time the sun was trying to come out, and as nature was slowly donning her autumn coat, the picture before them was one of golden glory rising from the golden bracken at ground level, up to the tops of the trees, and the secretive silence of the pine plantation was whispering all around them. A truly glorious experience.

They experienced some difficulty in locating Leighton Park Farm, as they had had to deviate from the actual path. Eventually they arrived, after twice asking directions, their way taking them past many pools including Offa's Pool, which in past days, was the reservoir for the Leighton Estate Waterworks. It was only 3.45 p.m. when they arrived at Gartheur Farm and Mrs Mostyn met them in her curlers and was obviously not quite ready, but they were warmly greeted with a cuppa and biscuits. It must be mentioned here that they actually saw a heron take off from the trout pool and fly up to his nest at the top of a very tall tree. The whole complex was most unusual; no village but a small community of farmhouses surrounded with the most beautiful historical barns and outhouses, some being in very good condition, but others obviously the worse for wear, and all very very old.

They were shown their rooms which looked very clean and comfortable, but there was definitely a chill in the air. The bathroom was absolutely huge and had obviously been converted; this unfortunately was located on the ground floor which would necessitate quite a long trek during the night, for anyone who found such a journey necessary. This always applied to C and M without any doubt. F seemed to be a little more fortunate – but not always ! There was no central heating, and the sheets were icy cold, but doubtless they would survive. After all, the builders of the Dyke had no such comforts, and as they were supposed to be following in their footsteps, all complaining must be dismissed from their thoughts! The supper was served at six o'clock consisting of very large pork cutlets, apple sauce, potatoes, carrots, peas and gravy, followed by apple pie and custard for C and cherry pie and custard for F and M. C could not resist the apple sauce which was left, so scoffed the lot accompanied by the custard. Not a thing was left but it was all scrumptious.

During the course of conversation with Mrs Mostyn, M timidly asked if it would be all right for them to go down to the bathroom in the night, as was their wont (she was actually thinking of the dog). Mrs Mostyn replied that there would be 'no need'. They were a little mystified by this remark, until they ascended to their respective bedrooms to find each one 'resplendent with pot'! They were very grateful, but felt it might be somewhat embarrassing trooping, via the kitchen to the bathroom, balancing their pots; so they braved the freezing conditions in the bathroom. Despite it all they had a warm and comfortable night. M kept warm by wearing C's thick red walking socks and looked an absolute fright; nobody saw what F got up to!.

The morning dawned fine and much clearer. Breakfast was served about eight o'clock – grapefruit, bacon, egg and tomato, toast and marmalade and oodles of tea – coffee for F. They were presented with three pieces of home-made sponge cake for elevenses. The dog was named Katie and the two cats: Tom and the Vicar – who was born with a white collar around his or her neck, plus a white front. The white collar had disappeared as age advanced but the name had stuck.

They left at nine o'clock; their way took them back through Leighton Woods, and after a steady climb for about a mile they regained the Offa's Dyke path, and the signpost pointing them up some very steep steps. From the track they had a very good view of Leighton Hall far below. On through the woods they went until they came to a lodge, inhabited by a very old man living entirely alone, who bred peacocks. He chatted to them and said that he hardly ever went out, just occasionally to Welshpool, but he had a friend to do his shopping. Absolute silence reigned there but he said that he was never lonely. Quite a stoic they decided. They had their elevenses by the side of the road there, and then on to the A490 near Forden, where they met a lone rambler walking for a week on the Dyke with his dog.

After leaving the road and crossing many fields, they suddenly heard much noise and squeaking coming from the garden of a house. They saw a proud peacock mum with her two babies plus a family of about four baby kittens all mewing frantically, the mother viewing them all from a distance with total unconcern. M made the mistake of picking up a little black one, who nestled

up to her purring loudly. Definitely love at first sight! However
they had to part, so Blackie was put into her own garden. This
didn't suit Blackie, who was determined to follow them; three
times they tried to put her into her own garden, but eventually C,
cursing under his breath at M's foolishness, marched determinedly
back down the path and placed Blackie with her own family and

Resting on the Dyke

hurried away like mad hoping Blackie this time would stay put.
They did not dare to look around to see what was happening, so
they would never know the fate of Blackie.

Lunch was eaten on the Dyke at 12.14; cheese and pate
sandwiches, Mars bars, etc., looking over a glorious view towards
Montgomery. They started walking again about one o'clock; a
very gentle walk that time across many fields alongside the Dyke.

They had an afternoon cuppa in a field by a wood overlooking Montgomery. They had made good time and it was only about 2.30 in the afternoon. They rested and gazed into the distance overwhelmed by the immenseness of the landscape, and the far reaching views of this thinly populated part of Wales.

They arrived in Montgomery at about 3.15; sat on a bench by the side of the road, and then toured a craft shop where M purchased two gifts, and then on to find Mrs Holloway in Market Square. This turned out to be a most beautiful old house which was re-thatched in 1771. The beams were all oak and the old oak doors had been taken out of Montgomery Castle. It was really warm and cosy and they sat by a glowing log fire whilst drinking a lovely cuppa. Mrs Holloway had been a widow for three years and did B&B for occupation and interest. She had one daughter, who had four daughters herself and one son. Mr and Mrs Holloway did have one son who had died at the age of sixteen. She also had a tortoiseshell puss named Felix, despite the fact that she was female and had just had four kittens!

Dinner was served at 5.15 consisting of vegetable soup, meat (M and C thought it was pork again, F decided it was rabbit), potatoes, mixed vegetables and cauliflower, followed by lemon meringue pie and cream. Whatever it was, everything was delicious. They became television addicts for a short while, watching the news and *Coronation Street*; prior to this they had been completely divorced from all current affairs. A blessed relief indeed! A further pot of tea saw them off to bed, and they all had a really comfortable night. The only danger here was the highly polished staircase, and they all had to negotiate this with the utmost care to avoid any further mishaps to their limbs.

They awoke to the same pattern of lovely weather and went down to breakfast at 8.30 a.m. Orange juice, bacon, egg and sausage, toast and marmalade. Mrs Holloway only charged them £7.50 each and M did say in great surprise, 'How very reasonable,' but she seemed quite satisfied and naturally C, F and M were.

On their way again through Montgomery – surely no town in Wales could match the charm of the Georgian houses, each one bearing a plaque giving the history and former use of the building. A few purchases were made and they actually started walking again at 9.50 a.m. They were able to take a slightly short cut through parkland to actually get on the path itself, which took them through a very large pheasantry with birds everywhere! Obviously being bred for the shoot, poor things! The 'going' was very easy that day, but they had their elevenses gazing at the formidable hills they were to encounter the following day. Once again they fell back on their maxim: 'Sufficient unto the day'.

As they had quite a lot of time on their hands they called in at the Bluebell Inn for drinks. This was run by a Miss Jones, and although it did not look terribly smart, it was quite a place. All the local doctors and dignitaries had their celebration lunches there, and they met some very friendly people who all looked a little aghast at their activities. Much excitement was caused by the felling of some enormous trees on the opposite corner, but eventually the job was completed without mishap.

On their way again through the most beautiful woods – a feature of this Autumn walk had been the abundance of berries and wild fruits blazing with colour all along their path – hips and haws, elderberries, holly and many luscious blackberries and the birds were all very busy feasting among them. (The birds were not the only eaters!) Gorse bushes abounded, some of which were still in flower and these, with the bushes of scarlet berries and their red and yellow leaves, made wonderful patches of colour in the sunshine. Some of the cottage walls too were covered with great splashes of crimson where the Virginia creeper had turned colour. On through Mellington Hall gateway, again into woodland, where they had their lunch. They reverted back to their childhood again playing 'I spy' as they had so much time to spare. A little robin came to pay his respects. On then to The Drewin, a most beautiful farmhouse standing high on top of a hill with views of the plain of Montgomery, Stiperstones and Long Mynd – all a little hazy at that time.

They arrived at about 3.45 p.m. but nobody was in and the place was quite deserted. It was beginning to get a little chilly so M poked around and discovered some barns and a few cows and a dog, and had made a mental note that maybe they would have to spend the night in one of them. A fervent prayer was uttered that this would not be the case, and to their great relief at five o'clock precisely, two cars zoomed up the drive and their fears were allayed. Mr and Mrs Richards were a lovely couple and had two lovely children; apparently they had all been to the dentist as it was their half-term.

Mrs Richards brightly asked, 'Do you want tea?'

M informed her that they were booked in for the night, and the look of absolute horror on Mrs Richard's face, told them quite plainly that they were totally unexpected! But in no time at all they were ushered into the sitting-room, a log fire was lit, they were regaled with a tray of tea and biscuits and began to warm up a little. They were later shown up to their bedrooms.

F's had hot and cold, television, heater and electric blanket. C and M's had heater and electric blanket and was beautifully and romantically furnished; the only unromantic part of the decor was C and M.

They were given a choice of evening meal, trout, pork steaks, steak, etc. Without thinking of anybody else's wishes M adamantly stated that she did not want trout, although she later learned that F loved it. Poor F. It was left to Mrs Richards to surprise them and once more pork steaks were served! Plenty of vegetables, cauliflower cheese, peas, carrots and potatoes, followed by raspberry sponge and cream. After dining they all sat by the log fire when the phone rang! No particular notice was taken of this common event until they were told that the call was for Mrs Shattock. Who on earth could it be, as nobody, absolutely nobody, knew of their whereabouts. With trepidation M took the phone to find that it was Mrs Holloway from Montgomery saying that she had forgotten to charge them for their evening meal! This was rather a blow, but mild in comparison to the calamities racing through M's mind. M promised to forward the necessary cheque on her return home.

They all had a glorious night in their glamorous surroundings, and came down to an early breakfast as they had a really long and hard day's walk before them. The usual substantial breakfast of bacon, egg, tomato and sausage, toast and marmalade. They set off in high spirits faced with a terrific climb of three hundred feet up to Kerry Hill Ridgeway. They encountered a huge bull over the brow of the hill so that he was completely hidden until they were right on top of him, but C, F, and M were of no interest to him fortunately. Another bull had to be passed on their descent to Mainstone, but as he was sitting down as they approached, they were quite ignorant of the fact until he stood up, just as F was passing, which caused quite a lot of consternation! They had their elevenses in the porch of Mainstone Church, and off again going up steeply, down steeply, very tough indeed. In fact that part of the path was reputed to be the toughest of the lot with which C, F and M, having done it, heartily agreed.

Lunch was eaten at 1.15 perched on sundry tree trunks at the top of a very steep hill. A lovely fresh wind was blowing but it was quite warm. They descended steeply into the Unk Valley which was a most beautiful place; not a farmhouse to be seen anywhere, just a river running at the bottom of the valley crossed by a small footbridge, and silence everywhere. It was a place that they would all love to visit again in the future. F found going downhill quite a strain on her legs so went down many of the slopes on her seat! The light was beginning to fade as they approached Newcastle, but as they could, by this time, see their route clearly below, they stopped for a very welcome cuppa. They still had to descend very steeply indeed through a belt of larch trees which looked so beautiful in their autumn glory.

On reaching Newcastle F and M took the shorter route to Newcastle Hall but C stuck to the path to Lower Spoad Farm and was delayed by getting mixed up with some sheep dipping activities, the farmer making the remark, 'This isn't *Emmerdale* you know.' However eventually they all met up with each other, and literally fell into the farmyard, glad to see Harriet awaiting them. It was lovely to get their boots off and don respectable shoes. They were soon settled inside with the usual welcoming pot of tea and coffee. There did seem to be a chill in the air and they felt truly grateful that the weather had just lasted out for them.

Newcastle Hall was a very old building, but elegantly furnished, warmed by a huge wood fire. Dinner was served in the huge dining hall and consisting of minestrone soup, pork, apple sauce, carrots, beans, potatoes, raspberries and cream followed by coffee in the lounge. They had hot and cold in bedrooms, the floors of the bedrooms seemed to slope in every direction but they all had a good night's rest although felt somewhat deflated that they had actually finished walking Offa's Dyke. They felt that they could easily walk on to Knighton, but sadly their holiday was over. They had to return home that day, having walked about 180 miles, taking the whole length of the path from north to south (168 miles) plus over six hundred stiles!

Breakfast was served at 8.30 a.m. – cornflakes, grapefruit, bacon, egg, tomato, fried bread and sausage, toast and marmalade. Mrs Reynolds had four children, three sons and one daughter, and six grandchildren yet was only a tiny slip of a thing.

They boarded Harriet at 9.45 and left in slight drizzle on their way to Knighton. The headquarters was approached with some fear that it might be closed as all was in darkness, but the reason for that was that Mrs Beech did not like fluorescent lighting. They proudly walked in and proffered their Walkers' Cards for checking. These were closely scrutinised by Mrs Beech who asked if she could keep them for her records but F and M badly wanted to keep theirs as souvenirs and mementos, so C came to the rescue and allowed her to retain his. They duly received their certificates, purchased cards, further badges, a plaque and 'the acorn' and after much hand-shaking and many congratulatory remarks, took their leave with a great sense of achievement. For the past two and a half years Offa's Dyke had been a constant subject of conversation, planning routes, booking accommodation, etc., etc., and it was hard to believe that it was all over and finished. But was it? C suggested the Pennine Way, but no way would F and M join him in that walk! Then they started to talk about 'doing the path the other way round'. What about the Wye Frontier Walk, the Diocesan Way, the Castles Route? Plenty still to go at. Time alone would tell but they all had a feeling in their bones that the Offa's Dyke country had not seen the last of them.

Rambling day after day was almost like a children's game, with its picnic meals and different sleeping places each night, in its sense of escape. It was the childishness of it that one enjoyed and the absolute freedom. But unfortunately games do not last – presently it was reality again.

C, F and M felt there was no countryside like the Border countryside because they had learned to love it so much. Its firm yet gentle lines of hill and dale, its deep valleys, its ordered confusion of features, its parkland and downland, its castles, its farm and ricks, and great barns and ancient trees; its pools and ponds, and shining threads of rivers, its flower-starred hedgerows, its orchards and woodland patches, its fields and winding lanes, its village greens and kindly inns and its abundant wild life.

Hopefully they would return!

An appropriate but accidental footnote was written by Margaret in March 1998:

> These days I have reached a back-packing watershed. My back hurts when I pick up my haversack and I feel like caving in, and have reached the stage when I actually prefer B&B to a youth hostel! But thank God I have been able to experience the utter freedom of walking in the country, forgetting about work, bills, etc., and just focus on the simple facts of living. Take it from me; there is no greater activity. It cannot even be found in a five-star hotel.

Glossary

pop eyes. Youngish attractive men (we think)

pieces. Usually refers to the fairer sex

Harriet. Their car

C.T.C. Cycling Touring Club

B.M.I. Birmingham Midland Institute

Y.H.A. Youth Hostelling Association

M. Margaret

D. Dora

C. Clive

F. Francis

H.F. Holiday Fellowship (we think)

F.T.B. Full to the brim

E.J.S. Ramblers. The Midland Area of the Rambler's Association 1930–1987

N.B. 'gay Irishman' has nothing to do with his sexuality!